Little Light

By **Alice Birch**

First performed at the Orange Tree Theatre, Richmond,
on 4 February 2015.

Little Light

By **Alice Birch**

Cast

Alison	**Lorna Brown**
Simon	**Paul Hickey**
Teddy	**Paul Rattray**
Clarissa	**Yolanda Kettle**

Creative

Writer	**Alice Birch**
Director	**David Mercatali**
Designer	**Madeleine Girling**
Lighting Designer	**Christopher Nairne**
Sound Designer	**Max Pappenheim**

CAST

LORNA BROWN
Alison

Lorna trained at Royal Central School of Speech and Drama.

Her work in theatre includes *Medea, Blurred Lines, Damned by Despair* (National Theatre); *Crowning Glory, The Big Life, Da Boyz, Funny Black Women on the Edge, Shoot 2 Win, One Dance Will Do* (Theatre Royal Stratford East); *Fear* (Bush Theatre); *Clybourne Park* (Royal Court/Wyndham's); *Short Fuses* (Bristol Old Vic); *Once On This Island* (Hackney Empire/tour); *Things of Dry Hours* (Royal Exchange/The Gate); *93.2FM* (Royal Court); *Trade* (RSC); *The Weave* (Soho Theatre); *Itsy Bitsy Spider, Anansi Steals the Wind* (Talawa); *Up Against the Wall* (Black Theatre Company); *Once On This Island* (West End).

TV includes *True Love, Holby City, Outnumbered, The Catherine Tate Show, Doctors, The Bill, The Vivienne Vyle Show, The Ronnie Ancona Show, Much Ado Nothing, French and Saunders, Family Business, Holby City, Jailbirds, Murder Most Horrid, Casualty, Dangerfield* and *Anna Lee*.

Film includes *Lady in the Van, Taking Stock, Les Misérables, Gambit, World War Z* and *Little Soldier* (Robert Award nomination).

PAUL HICKEY
Simon

Paul Hickey's recent theatre includes Nick Payne's *Incognito* (HighTide/Bush); *Children of the Sun* (National) and *The Last Yankee* (PrintRoom). Other work includes *Our Class, Peer Gynt, Romeo & Juliet* and *The Playboy of the Western World* (National Theatre); *Bang Bang Bang* and *O Go My Man* (Royal Court /Out of Joint); *Fewer Emergencies* and *Crazyblackmuthafuckinself* (Royal Court); *In the Next Room or The Vibrator Play* (Theatre Royal Bath); *Ghosts* (Arcola); *Fred's Diner* and *Wallenstein* (Chichester); *The Merchant of Venice* (RSC World Tour); *Faith Healer* (Hong Kong Arts Festival); *Protestants* (Soho Theatre); *Fall* (Traverse); *Drink Dance Laugh and Lie* (Bush); *In A Little World of Our Own* and *Pentecost* (Donmar); *The Ash Fire, Lady Windermere's Fan* and *Red Roses and Petrol* (Tricycle); *My Night with Reg* and *Dealer's Choice* (Birmingham Rep); *The Silver Tassie, The Plough and the Stars, Aristocrats, Howling Moons, Silent Sons* (Abbey Theatre); *Shiver* and *Spokesong* (Rough Magic).

TV includes *Critical, Doctor Who, Whitechapel, Sunshine, The Inspector Lynley Mysteries* (Series IV, V & VI), *Nuremburg, Friends and Crocodiles, Murder City, Rebel Heart, The Informant, Father Ted* and *The American*.

Film includes *A Hundred Streets, The Devil's Harvest, Noble, The Matchmaker, Wonder, Though the Sky Falls, On the Edge, Saving Private Ryan, Moll Flanders, Nora, Spin the Bottle, The General* and *Ordinary Decent Criminal*.

PAUL RATTRAY
Teddy

Paul's work in theatre includes *Romeo and Juliet* (Sherman Theatre, Cardiff); *Wonderland* (Hampstead); *Macbeth* (Perth Theatre/Tron, Glasgow); *Facts* (Finborough); *Three Sisters, In the Blue* (Young Vic); *Racing Demon, The Long and the Short and the Tall* (Sheffield Crucible); *Ditch* (Old Vic/High Tide); *Black Watch* (National Theatre of Scotland – world tour including the Barbican and New York); *Ravenhill for Breakfast, East Coast Chicken Supper, Shimmer* (Traverse); *The Shawl* (Arcola); *Dinner* (National Theatre); *Decky Does a Bronco* (Grid Iron); *The Anatomist* (Royal Lyceum, Edinburgh); *Hand Bag* (Actors Touring Company); *Playing the Game* (Jacknife).

TV includes *Holby City, Birdsong, Doctors, Last Rights, Casualty* and *The Bill*.

Film includes *Creep, Enigma, Max, Mike Bassett: England Manager* and *Morvin Caller*.

YOLANDA KETTLE
Clarissa

Yolanda trained at LAMDA.

Her work in theatre includes *Coolatully* (Finborough); *Birdland, Anhedonia* (Royal Court); *A Tale of Two Cities* (Royal & Derngate, Northampton); *A Doll's House* (Young Vic/Duke of York's); *Pride and Prejudice* (Open Air Regent's Park); *Hello/ Goodbye* (Hampstead); *The Seagull* (Arcola); *Saved* (Royal Court Gala).

TV includes *Father Brown, Mega Tsunami, Doctors, Holby City*.

Radio includes *A Change in The Willows*.

CREATIVE

ALICE BIRCH
Writer

Alice was the co-winner of the 2014 George Devine Award for *Revolt. She Said. Revolt Again.* (RSC, playing at The Other Place, Royal Court Theatre and Latitude Festival), winner of the Arts Foundation Award for Playwriting 2014, and was one of the BBC Writersroom 10 for 2014.

Writing includes *Little on the inside* (Almeida / Clean Break); *So Much Once* (24 Hour Celebrity Gala Old Vic); *Open Court Soap Opera* (Royal Court); *Salt* (Comedie de Valence) and *Flying the Nest* (BBC Radio 4). She is currently under commission to Clean Break, Pentabus Theatre, Young Vic, Royal Court Theatre and National Theatre; and is screenwriter in one of final selected filmmaking teams for this year's iFeatures scheme.

DAVID MERCATALI
Director

David is Associate Director at Southwark Playhouse.

Credits include Philip Ridley's *Tender Napalm*, for which he was nominated for the *Evening Standard* Outstanding Newcomer Award 2011, *Feathers in the Snow*, *Johnny Got His Gun* (Southwark Playhouse); Fringe First award winning *Dark Vanilla Jungle* (Pleasance, Edinburgh Fringe and Soho Theatre); *Coolatully*, *Black Jesus* (Finborough Theatre); *Sochi 2014* (Hope Theatre); *Someone to Blame* (King's Head Theatre); the premiere of Philip Ridley's *Moonfleece* (Riverside Studios and National Tour); *People's Day* (Pleasance, Islington); *Runners – the Return* (Underbelly, Edinburgh Fringe); *Weights*, and his own play, *The Sound* (Blue Elephant Theatre).

He has also developed new work with Paines Plough, the Finborough and Theatre503 and will next be directing Philip Ridley's new play, *Radiant Vermin*, at the Bristol Tobacco Factory and Soho Theatre.

MADELEINE GIRLING
Designer

Madeleine won The Linbury Prize for Stage Design 2013 and The Lord Williams Memorial Prize for Design 2012. She trained at The Royal Welsh College of Music and Drama in 2012.

Designs include *The Chronicles of Kaliki* (The Gate); *Time and the Conways, Arcadia* (Nottingham Playhouse); Alice Birch's *Revolt. She Said. Revolt Again* and *The Ant and the Cicada* (RSC Midsummer Mischief Festival); *Gardening for the Unfulfilled* and *Alienated* (Latitude/Edinburgh Festival); *How to Curse, Tender Napalm* (Bristol Old Vic Theatre School); *A Welshman's Guide to Breaking-Up* (Cardiff); *Hey Diddle Diddle* (Bristol Old Vic); *Blood Wedding* (The Bute Theatre, Cardiff); and *The Ducks* (SEArED/Pleasance, Edinburgh).

Other work includes prop and puppet assistant for *A Midsummer Night's Dream* (Bristol Old Vic/Handspring); set and costume design assistant: *Wild Oats, The Life After* (Bristol Old Vic). Prop maker: *Phantom of the Opera* (Cardiff); set assistant and puppet maker: *Solomon* (European Live Arts Network, Fuecchio, Italy); and set assistant on *The Passion* (Wildworks/National Theatre Wales). Scenic art for the film *Da Vinci's Demons*. Art Department Assistant: *Skins* (Channel 4).

CHRISTOPHER NAIRNE
Lighting Designer

Christopher has previously worked with David Mercatali on *Coolatully* (Finborough Theatre*), Johnny Got His Gun* and *Our Ajax* (Southwark Playhouse).

Other recent theatre work includes *Lionboy* (Complicite - Tricycle Theatre & international tour); *Around the World in 80 Days* (Cambridge Junction); *Sense and Sensibility* (Watermill Theatre, Newbury); *Cans* (Theatre503); *The School for Scandal* (Park Theatre & Theatre Royal, Bury); *Dracula* (for Theatre Royal Bath); *The Ghost Hunter* (UK tour); *Fiesta: The Sun Also Rises* (Trafalgar Studios); *Shallow Slumber* (Soho Theatre); *A Dish of Tea with Dr Johnson* (Out of Joint - Arts Theatre & UK tour).

Opera includes *Vivienne* (Linbury Studio, Royal Opera House); *Facade/Eight Songs for a Mad King* and *The Impresario* (Melos Sinfonia); *The Adventures of Count Ory* (Blackheath Halls Opera); *Belshazzar* (Trinity Laban Conservatoire); *Albert Herring* and *La Calisto* (Hampstead Garden Opera); *Albert Herring* (Surrey Opera); *The Cunning Little Vixen* (Ryedale Festival Opera); *La Bohème* (OperaUpClose; 2011 Olivier Award winner).

For a full list of credits, please see www.christophernairne.co.uk

MAX PAPPENHEIM
Sound Designer

Max's theatre credits include *The Distance* (Orange Tree Theatre); *Toast, The Man Who Shot Liberty Valance, The Archimedes Principle* (Park); *Usagi Yojimbo, Johnny Got His Gun, Three Sisters, Fiji Land, Our Ajax* (Southwark Playhouse); *Mrs Lowry and Son* (Trafalgar Studios); *CommonWealth* (Almeida); *Ghost, Strangers On A Train* (English Theatre, Frankfurt); *Rachel, This Was A Man, Martine, Variation on a Theme, Black Jesus, Somersaults, The Fear of Breathing* (Finborough Theatre); *The Faction Rep Season 2015, Das Ding* (New Diorama); *The Hotel Plays* (Defibrillator at the Langham); *Being Tommy Cooper* (National Tour); *Shipwrecked!, The Mystery of Irma Vep, Borderland, Kafka v Kafka* (Brockley Jack); *Freefall* (New Wimbledon Studio); *Four Corners One Heart* (Theatre503); *Awkward Conversations with Animals I've F*cked* (Underbelly, Edinburgh); *Below the Belt* (Pleasance, Edinburgh).

As Associate credits include *The Island* (Young Vic); *Fleabag* (Soho).

Nominated for OffWestEnd Awards 2012 and 2014 for Best Sound Designer.

LITTLE LIGHT

Alice Birch

LITTLE LIGHT

OBERON BOOKS
LONDON

WWW.OBERONBOOKS.COM

First published in 2015 by Oberon Books Ltd
521 Caledonian Road, London N7 9RH
Tel: +44 (0) 20 7607 3637 / Fax: +44 (0) 20 7607 3629
e-mail: info@oberonbooks.com
www.oberonbooks.com

Visit www.oberonbooks.com to read more about all our books
and to buy them. You will also find features, author interviews and
news of any author events, and you can sign up for e-newsletters
so that you're always first to hear about our new releases.

For my sister, Rosa.

Thanks to Giles, Sam, Jude, David Mercatali, Paul Miller,
Lorna, Yolanda, Paul R and Paul H – and the many more
who read the play out loud and in their heads.

Six-year-old thanks are owed to David Eldridge
for your challenge and for your kindness.

Little Light was first performed at the Orange Tree Theatre, Richmond, on 4 February 2015 with the following cast:

ALISON	Lorna Brown
TEDDY	Paul Rattray
CLARISSA	Yolanda Kettle
SIMON	Paul Hickey

Director	David Mercatali
Designer	Madeleine Girling
Lighting Designer	Christopher Nairne
Sound Designer	Max Pappenheim

**Orange
Tree
Theatre**

Characters

ALISON

TEDDY

CLARISSA

SIMON

/ Denotes the overlapping of speech.

Words in square brackets [ ] are not spoken.

The absence of a full stop at the end of a line denotes
a kind of interruption – the lines should run at speed.

The use of a full stop on a line on its own suggests a pause –
whether this is a single beat or ten minutes
depends on what feels right.

The spacing of the dialogue, the use of upper and lower case
letters and the punctuation is all there to help the actor in
terms of the pacing and the weight of their words.

There are no stairs.

ALISON has just walked in. She is soaking wet.

TEDDY can hear a bird.

TEDDY   Think of the light.

                   .

ALISON   Fuck.

TEDDY   Imagine all that light.

                   .

ALISON   Fuck.

TEDDY   You know how people always talk about light
                   just sort of

                   Flooding

                   a room – on on [TV] and in in [films] and I'm
                   I'm sceptical to be honest because it's well it's
                   it's bollocks isn't it – but

                   But it does.

                   It drenches it. We are literally Wading in light.

ALISON   .

                   You are an absolute tit

TEDDY   It's

                   Incredible.

ALISON   Are you drunk?

TEDDY   I was thinking about spiral staircases

ALISON   Seriously – are you a little bit hammered?

TEDDY   You always said you wanted a spiral staircase

ALISON   What

9

TEDDY	So
ALISON	Seriously – when did
TEDDY	I wanted to give you a spiral staircase.
	So.
ALISON	That. Teddy.
	Is a fucking Ladder
TEDDY	It is a work in progress
ALISON	So. So let me get this. Let me. Because this is – so. You wanted to give me a spiral / staircase
TEDDY	/ staircase, yes – yes I wanted to give
ALISON	So you ripped out my perfectly functioning staircase and you are – what – you are essentially Showing me a ladder I already had – and and – when the When did we even have a conversation about spiral fucking staircases
TEDDY	All the time – you talk about it All the time
ALISON	Are you – No I. When – When do
TEDDY	You talked about it three weeks ago
ALISON	No I
TEDDY	And in Venice. When we were in Venice you didn't stop going on about
ALISON	You're trying to wind me up – you are inexplicably trying to get a a
TEDDY	The whole way round that little shit piazza you
ALISON	Rise out of me for some unknown – We have never been to fucking Venice
TEDDY	Yes we have
ALISON	You have lost your Fucking Mind

TEDDY	We go all the time
ALISON	Jesus Christ
TEDDY	How would I know about the little shit piazza if We hadn't been to Venice
ALISON	How would you know about the unspecific Italian word for Square you just dragged / out of your brain
TEDDY	/ Are you thinking about the dinner parties?
ALISON	.

TEDDY sees the guests. Smiles at them.

TEDDY	Are you thinking about the dinner parties?
ALISON	I'm thinking about my fucking stairs
TEDDY	It's these WINDOWS. They're Giants – and and it's really funny
ALISON	is it
TEDDY	It's really Stupid because I never really Noticed them before but they're Ridiculous and We – We could throw these really really shit dinner parties and it wouldn't matter because come sunset okay – come sunset we'd turn to our guests – our food-poisoned guests and be like FUCK YOU. Sunset. See that. Sunset.
ALISON	Right.

ALISON is close to tears.

Are you

Right.

You.

Because I'm just going to

And pretend that none of that

.

I think this is.

Nothing. Um. Nothing is really as it should be and. And. You are. Knocking my.

And.

And I'm. I'm. I think I'm.

.

TEDDY   It keeps banging into things

ALISON   Okay.

         What.

TEDDY   The light.

ALISON   .

         The light

TEDDY   Light. Yes.

ALISON   Teddy

TEDDY   It keeps.

         It keeps banging into things – into stairs and walls and doors and and things

         The phone rings.

         and. And they just keep getting in the way.

         And. It was.

         The phone rings.

         It was

         The phone rings.

It was

The phone rings.

It was

The phone stops.

It was

Beep.

A breath and a click.

When you were gone – I couldn't sleep – not
at all, not even a bit actually and and I know
people Say that but and it's I'm I'm lying there
and it's like it just hit me, I keep thinking that if
we just open it up a bit, we could let it all out.
All of this light.

It's like. I've found this little burst of light in
a very small box within a bigger box within a
bigger box and I need to to let it out.

ALISON	Okay.
	Okay. I. So.
	I shouldn't have gone away – I
TEDDY	No, it's
ALISON	I clearly shouldn't have gone away and this is your way of of – but okay, I shouldn't have gone away
TEDDY	don't say
ALISON	And it's just. It's just that You said it would be fine and
TEDDY	It will be
ALISON	You were the one that Said it would be fine and and

TEDDY	And it will
ALISON	And this is – this is Enormous actually Teddy because you said that – you said that you Got that and
TEDDY	Come on Ali
ALISON	No – because it's. It's just that it's a little bit fucking shit. Your timing. Teddy.
TEDDY	Okay
ALISON	No not Okay
TEDDY	Alright
ALISON	Because – Actually, Teddy, I don't really give a shit. No, no – honestly
TEDDY	fine
ALISON	Do whatever you like – Seriously – I don't give – because you – Gut our house as much as you like until we're sliding down walls and into the sea but today
TEDDY	yep
ALISON	Today is not the day to be today I need you to
TEDDY	It will look
ALISON	I need you to just Stop actually and
TEDDY	Better – it will Look better.
	You know. That it will look better
ALISON	Oh my God, Teddy
TEDDY	That's the house – that is the beauty of this house – you always said that – We always said
ALISON	We always said
TEDDY	That it had Potential

ALISON	In Venice did we say that
TEDDY	We said that it had Potential and and that's one of those things you just say but actually fucking actually – it really does
ALISON	Feel like I'm going a bit nuts now Teddy
TEDDY	If you just Looked though – if you would just
ALISON	Feel like I'm going completely nuts now
TEDDY	if you would just Look at it for one second and stop being such a shit you would see that it will look better – miles better
ALISON	You're not listening! You're not listening or engaging with rational thought at all though because that is not the fucking point
TEDDY	What is the point then?
	.
ALISON	Are you
	.
	What's the – did you just ask what's
	.
TEDDY	Do you want me to put the stairs back up
ALISON	No I don't want you to put them back up, I want you to have not knocked them down in the first place – I just Asked you to make lunch, I just asked if you could make lunch – You Offered, in fact, I would do the rest and you would make fucking lunch and you've ripped your stupid staircase
TEDDY	Our stairs
ALISON	No your stairs, your stupid stupid stairs

TEDDY	I was very gentle with her.
	.
ALISON	Did you make any lunch?
TEDDY	Yes.
ALISON	What?
TEDDY	What?
ALISON	What did you make
TEDDY	Lunch. Just some lunch.
ALISON	Right. What is it though
TEDDY	It's fine. It's lunch
ALISON	Stop saying lunch
TEDDY	That's what I made. Lunch
ALISON	What does it consist of, Teddy
TEDDY	Fish pie.
ALISON	Fish pie?
TEDDY	Yes. Fish pie.
ALISON	What happened to the lamb?
TEDDY	The.
	Nothing Happened to the lamb – I just thought fish pie would be nice
ALISON	Fish pie and no stairs. Very nice.
TEDDY	I couldn't find the recipe. You hadn't left it out.
ALISON	I hadn't
TEDDY	You hadn't left the recipe out. So I made fish pie.
ALISON	We never have – why would you make a

I hadn't left it

TEDDY   Are you alright

ALISON   I just. I put it on the fridge. Teddy.

TEDDY   Our fridge?

ALISON   Yes. Yes our fridge. I put the recipe on our
fridge.

TEDDY   The actual recipe? You cut the recipe for lamb
out of the book and put it on our fridge?

ALISON   No.

     .

TEDDY   Are you okay?

ALISON   Yes. It's just that I. I photocopied it and put it on
the fridge – on Our fridge and

TEDDY   How

     How did you put it on fridge?

ALISON   Underneath a magnet. Teddy.

TEDDY   Of course.

     .

     Alison.

     The phone rings.

ALISON   We don't have time. I don't have time. For this.

     The phone rings.

     ALISON picks up the phone.

     Hello?

     .

     Hello?

She hangs up. Makes a face.

What's that smell?

TEDDY	Who was on the phone
ALISON	Did you hear me talking to anyone – Teddy, that better not be lunch, your fish pie better not be making that smell, that Old old smell
TEDDY	You said Hello and then hung up – that doesn't mean they didn't say anything
ALISON	They didn't – what Is that
TEDDY	It's the compost – it's just the – I'll take it out
ALISON	Why is the Compost in here
TEDDY	I was on my way out with it when you
ALISON	Why didn't you take it out the back door – what is Wrong with you
TEDDY	I'll do it – I was on my way out with it and you came back and here we fucking are
ALISON	You were on your way out with the compost
TEDDY	I had a lot to do
ALISON	Ripping my house up
TEDDY	Jesus Christ
ALISON	I just don't understand why you didn't do the lamb – you Know that's what we have
TEDDY	I told you – you didn't leave the recipe out
ALISON	I left it on the fridge
TEDDY	where I could see it – you didn't leave it out where I could see it
ALISON	It's On the Fridge – how could I have left it More Out

TEDDY	I didn't see it okay – I didn't see it and I'm sorry but fish pie
ALISON	I told you that was where I would leave it
TEDDY	is nice okay, fish pie will be
ALISON	I did Tell you I would leave it on the fridge so how you
TEDDY	When? When did you tell me
ALISON	In the note.
	On the hall table.
	The note that I left you. On the table in the hall. With the name of the hotel.
TEDDY	Oh.
ALISON	And when to take the bins out. Recycling on Wednesday, green bin
TEDDY	Yep. Yes. Yep
ALISON	Defrost the lamb. Recipe on the fridge.
TEDDY	Right.
	.
ALISON	Teddy.
TEDDY	Yep.
ALISON	Did you read the note?
TEDDY	What?
ALISON	Did you read that note? The note in the hallway. The one with 'Teddy' written in massive letters at the top?
TEDDY	Oh.
	No.

ALISON	Right.

.

Shit.

.

This is. This is all wrong.

None of it is

That's.

TEDDY	Ali.
ALISON	It's fucked
TEDDY	It's not
ALISON	It's done
TEDDY	Ali, don't – it'll be
ALISON	fucked. It's fucked it's fucked it's fucked
TEDDY	I
ALISON	O.

.

That's it, isn't it?

It's not going to happen, is it?

| TEDDY | Ali |
| ALISON | I think it's because I know that this isn't – I Do know. I Do know that this is for me and not. But. Every other day of the year, Teddy, it's not about me and. |

.

I.

| TEDDY | I'll fix it |

ALISON	No
TEDDY	I will. I'll do it – I'll fix it I'll.
	Let me fix it for you.
	Let me put it back together.
	Ali.
ALISON	.
	I'm tired.
	.
TEDDY	It's our shell.
	Remember? It's our house sitting on our beach. Our lovely shell house.
	With its lovely white bones.
	And we'll gut it and we'll peel it and we'll take its very middle out, out towards its shell bones, its lovely lovely light. And we'll fill it. With you. And me. And us. And all that we have made.
	Hello.
	Remember?
	.
ALISON	I'm soaking.
	.

ALISON climbs the ladder. Leaves the room.

Sound of a shower running.

TEDDY tidies the room, lays the table for three. Brings in a colander of peas and a colander with apples.

This can take some time.

TEDDY can hear the sound of a bird, loud now.

Doorbell.

TEDDY stops.

The noise of the water stops.

Doorbell.

TEDDY   Ali?

.

Al?

Someone begins to bang on the front door. Loud.

TEDDY can't move.

Banging.

He exits into the kitchen.

Doorbell.

ALISON comes onto the landing wrapped in a towel. She stops at the top of the ladder.

Sound of the front door opening.

CLARISSA, soaking wet and heavily pregnant rushes in, holding a bunch of sweetpeas. She walks quickly into the centre of the room, she doesn't see ALISON. CLARISSA never really touches her very protruding bump.

CLARISSA   I.

Shit.

Hello?

She pulls her boots off.

Hello? Ted? Ali?

She looks around. Looks up. Sees ALISON. Starts.

Fucking hell – you scared the crap out of –

Ali.

Jesus.

What're you

The door was open – it was

Wide Open and

I didn't. I wanted to – God, what're you Doing?
Standing there like a fucking – my heart is going
like a – and. You look nice. And.

She laughs.

Shit. You're making me.

.

You shouldn't Do that – you shouldn't just leave
front doors wide open, there could literally be
maniacs round the – that's not funny, is it, I'm
not being – I'm Pissing you off already aren't I
and I'm – I've only just

Look. Ali. I wanted to. I wanted to

Fuck – this is hard – this is really hard, this is
why they should Encourage you to drink and
take substances, not Abstain, it's really – nine
months is really – I just. I wanted to ask you if
this year

Could be different. Perhaps.

And. It's just with the. With the – I feel a bit like
this year Has to be different and we could Let it.
Couldn't we.

I ran. I ran all the way up the track to ask you to
just.

Stop it now.

ALISON	You're early.
CLARISSA	Okay. Did you hear me?
ALISON	You're wet. You're dripping everywhere
CLARISSA	Did you actually listen to what I said?
	Did you get Any of my messages?
ALISON	Why are you Gabbling
CLARISSA	Did you. Can you hear me up there or –
	It's. It's just that we've done this. We've done it
ALISON	Yes
CLARISSA	And I'm asking you Not to do it
ALISON	You're not Asking, you're talking At me. It's really irritating
CLARISSA	Okay – look, you have Choices okay. We all have the potential to make Choices all the time and you don't have to do this – you could Choose to be different
ALISON	Everyone's being a fuck up today.
	Look at what Teddy did.
CLARISSA	Please, Alison.
ALISON	I need to get changed
CLARISSA	Did you hear what I said about Choices
ALISON	Try not to flood everywhere Clarissa
	ALISON exits.
CLARISSA	I might do. I might just break my fucking waters all over your sofa – Alison.
	CLARISSA puts a fist inside her mouth.

Her phone rings, loudly.

She lets it ring off.

TEDDY enters.

Hello.

.

There was no answer. I rang the bell.

I Banged.

The door was just. Wide open.

TEDDY	Right?
CLARISSA	It's raining
TEDDY	You're soaked through
CLARISSA	That would be the rain
TEDDY	You're really early
CLARISSA	Yes
TEDDY	You're never early
CLARISSA	No
TEDDY	You're not an early person
CLARISSA	Well – no
TEDDY	Your coat
CLARISSA	It's fine
TEDDY	It's soaking
CLARISSA	Because of the rain
TEDDY	You'll get a cold
CLARISSA	I never get colds
TEDDY	You always got colds

CLARISSA	It's fine – I'm fine, I quite like it
TEDDY	The cold
CLARISSA	Why's there a ladder just in the middle of your house
TEDDY	Was that your phone?
CLARISSA	What
TEDDY	A minute ago. Ringing – I heard something. Was it your phone?
CLARISSA	I don't know
TEDDY	Ringing, could swear there was a ringing
CLARISSA	Heard nothing out here
TEDDY	Wasn't yours
CLARISSA	Mine's dead
TEDDY	Has she seen you
CLARISSA	She's Cross.
	We didn't get much of a – but it doesn't. Teddy. I wanted to say
TEDDY	Tea? Do you want something to drink?
CLARISSA	No, thank you
TEDDY	something hot – you need something warm
CLARISSA	No, I really
TEDDY	A towel, you need
CLARISSA	No
TEDDY	You're soaked through – you need
CLARISSA	I don't Need – I don't Need anything, Teddy
	Nothing – not a thing, except. To Talk to you

TEDDY	Look at you.
	Just. Jesus.
	Look at you.
CLARISSA	I know – Teddy
TEDDY	I knocked the stairs down
CLARISSA	I want it to be. I want
TEDDY	That's why she's cross
CLARISSA	I want it to be. Normal.
TEDDY	The door was Wide open?
CLARISSA	Different.
	If we. Teddy, if you and I can Make her – help her – help her, I meant Help, if we can help her see then.
	.
	Teddy.
TEDDY	You're dripping everywhere.
	TEDDY exits into the kitchen.
CLARISSA	That doesn't
	CLARISSA's phone rings again.
	She silences it.
	TEDDY re-enters with towels. He passes some to CLARISSA. She holds them.
TEDDY	You look
	You look well, you look really. Great. How are you?
CLARISSA	I'm fine.

I'm fine, thank you – I'm, yes, I'm well.

I'm early – I'm sorry about. I did try to call. But you never fucking answer your phones

TEDDY   No?

CLARISSA   All of yesterday. And the day before. And the day before. I called. For three days

TEDDY   I'm sorry

CLARISSA   I left messages

TEDDY   I don't check them – I'm not good with

CLARISSA   What's the point in having a phone if

TEDDY   Can you just

for a second? My head is.

.

You should sit down.

CLARISSA   I don't want to

TEDDY   Do people tell you what to do all the time

CLARISSA   She's very heavy

TEDDY   .

She?

CLARISSA   Simon likes Victoria. And Charlotte. And Elizabeth.

TEDDY   Fuck.

CLARISSA   I know

TEDDY   No – I meant. A girl. That's really. It's just.

.

Great.

CLARISSA	I emailed Alison when I found out. Months ago. A few times.
	Perhaps she forgot
TEDDY	And how is um how is Simon?
CLARISSA	Excited.
	He keeps building things.
TEDDY	That's nice.
CLARISSA	All the walls are lemon yellow
TEDDY	right
CLARISSA	Big big bunches of flowers everywhere and and rocking horses and
TEDDY	course
CLARISSA	and tiny furniture for all these small humans he seems to think I'll just keep producing but
TEDDY	Well. Who knows.
CLARISSA	I can't see this one yet.
TEDDY	No.
CLARISSA	Is your head – Can I talk about something properly now or

ALISON enters and climbs down the ladder.

Alison

ALISON	The shower's broken. The water's cold.
TEDDY	Doesn't mean it's broken
CLARISSA	I've been trying to ask you both something
ALISON	I thought. I thought that we could just start a bit earlier than normal.
	Take our time.

	Do it properly.
	Catch up.
CLARISSA	No.
ALISON	We could have some tea
TEDDY	She doesn't want tea
CLARISSA	He's right – I don't want tea
ALISON	Just a cup of tea
	The phone rings.
CLARISSA	I don't want any
ALISON	It's not a big deal, Clarissa, it's just tea
CLARISSA	And I'm fine – are you going to get that?
	The phone rings.
	Do you not answer your phone to anyone then?
ALISON	it doesn't have to Mean anything other than tea
CLARISSA	I still don't want any
	Thank you.
	The phone clicks.
	ALISON sits down. She starts shelling peas.
	.
	Something herbal then
TEDDY	We've got
	fennel
	green tea, cammomile
CLARISSA	I don't care.
	Thank you.

TEDDY exits into the kitchen.

ALISON   Sit down. You look lost.

               CLARISSA sits.

               Your coat is wet.

CLARISSA   I don't mind it

ALISON   You're making a mess

               .

               CLARISSA takes her coat off.

               Are you planning on stealing those?

CLARISSA   Yes. Yes, I'm planning on stealing your tea towels.

               Teddy gave them to me.

ALISON   Apples or peas?

CLARISSA   lent or. Not gave. To dry myself.

ALISON   .

               You always have apples.

               Apples.

               I know you're not one for manual labour but it's not difficult.

               Would you rather shell peas?

               .

               Okay.

               Alright.

               Since you're so early.

               What.

CLARISSA   I don't think we should do this.

ALISON   Okay.

CLARISSA   I really don't think that we need to do this.

ALISON   How're things, Clarissa?

CLARISSA   There's no Need

ALISON   No need

CLARISSA   There isn't – you can make a choice

ALISON   Thank you and how is Simon?

CLARISSA   Please, Alison

ALISON   Question, Clarissa, answer a question when it's asked, how is Simon

CLARISSA   He's fine – Alison

ALISON   Oh good, and work

CLARISSA   I'm not working

ALISON   Of course, why would you work

CLARISSA   I'm on maternity leave – Alison, please

ALISON   Why are you Asking, Clarissa? Why are you bothering to Ask?

             .

CLARISSA   Because. Because you Know that this is. That unless you say, I won't. I'll.

             Because if you say we're doing this then

             Then of course we're doing this – but

             I'm asking for it to be different.

             .

ALISON   Apples, Clarissa.

             .

CLARISSA	.

CLARISSA's phone rings.

ALISON	What's that
CLARISSA	It's my phone
ALISON	I know it's your phone, what are you doing with it on
CLARISSA	I forgot. Shit. I. I don't usually get signal. Here. I
ALISON	Turn it off
CLARISSA	It's Simon
ALISON	Turn it off
CLARISSA	It's Simon
ALISON	I don't give a shit turn it off
CLARISSA	Alison
ALISON	Turn it off
CLARISSA	It's just a phone
ALISON	Turn it off – just turn it off turn it off
CLARISSA	It's off it's off it's off
	Jesus.
	It's off. See.
	.

TEDDY enters with tea – passes it around.

CLARISSA starts to peel apples.

The phone rings.

They look at it.

TEDDY unplugs it.

CLARISSA	Are you
TEDDY	Lunch won't be too long. It's not far off
CLARISSA	Did you just Unplug your phone?
TEDDY	It's a very straightforward recipe
ALISON	Why don't you sit? Why is everyone hovering?

TEDDY sits.

.

TEDDY stands up again.

CLARISSA's phone rings.

.

.

CLARISSA	I'm sorry, but it's Simon and if I don't pick up he will freak out
ALISON	I don't care
CLARISSA	and and call the police or something – he does that you know, he actually did that once
ALISON	I don't care turn it off now, you don't have a
CLARISSA	it won't be a big thing
ALISON	phone you didn't have a fucking phone, why're you being such a

The doorbell rings.

.

It rings again.

TEDDY moves towards the hall.

What're you doing?

TEDDY	Answering the door. There's someone at the door.
ALISON	I know there's someone at the door Teddy.
	So?
TEDDY	So. What if they want something? If they want to come in?
ALISON	If they want to come in?
	Are you
	We're busy
	They can't fucking come in
TEDDY	What if they keep ringing
ALISON	I don't care
	Doorbell.
TEDDY	They might just keep on ringing
	Someone bangs on the front door.
ALISON	They'll go away
TEDDY	They might not
ALISON	They'll give up
SIMON	*(Off.)* Hello? Hello?
TEDDY	*(Calling.)* Who is it?
ALISON	Teddy
SIMON	*(Off.)* It's Simon.
	Simon Harper.
	I'm looking for Clarissa?
	.

ALISON	Clarissa.
	Simon Harper is here and apparently he's looking for you
TEDDY	Your Simon is here?
	SIMON knocks on the door.
ALISON	I can't. No. I can't really believe that this is
SIMON	*(Off.)* Hello? Clarissa? Teddy?
TEDDY	We have to let him in
ALISON	Why is he here, Clarissa?
	.
	No?
	Nothing?
TEDDY	Alison
SIMON	*(Off.)* Cliss? Babe, are you okay?
ALISON	I could laugh. Really. I could laugh.
	CLARISSA's phone rings.
SIMON	*(Off.)* Okay. Okay, I can hear your phone
	And
	Getting a bit worried now
	CLARISSA silences her phone.
	Look, I don't want to break anyone's door down but
ALISON	What were you thinking
TEDDY	We have to let him in
ALISON	Were you thinking

TEDDY	We have to let him in
ALISON	I Know we have to let him in, Teddy, I am just trying to prepare myself for this monumental fuck up

.

SIMON	*(Off.)* Cliss
ALISON	[Fine. Go.]

TEDDY exits into the hallway.

CLARISSA	Look, he knows
ALISON	She speaks
CLARISSA	He understands
ALISON	Does he really
CLARISSA	Look, Ali
ALISON	All of it
CLARISSA	There's just

Sound of a door being unlocked.

He knows so there's really no point in in

Sound of a door being opened.

ALISON	I think there's every point

Sound of TEDDY and SIMON greeting one another.

CLARISSA	I'm asking you. I am asking – no, okay, I'm begging you not to do this Ali
ALISON	You haven't come all this way
	With your belly
	All this way
	For us not to honour tradition, Clarissa.

That would be terribly fucking rude.

Terribly cruel of you.

.

CLARISSA   Please

ALISON   I can't believe you're still Asking for things.

             TEDDY enters with SIMON in tow. SIMON is soaking,
             very muddy, holding a bottle of wine and a soggy cake
             box. He goes to CLARISSA.

SIMON   Are you okay?

CLARISSA   I'm fine

SIMON   Are you sure?

CLARISSA   Simon, I'm

SIMON   Don't do that – don't shrug me off – are you
             okay?

CLARISSA   I'm fine

SIMON   Look at me

CLARISSA   Simon

SIMON   What the hell happened?

CLARISSA   Simon, this is my sister, Alison.

             .

SIMON   Of course, sorry. Great to finally meet you. At
             last.

             .

             Sorry I'm such a mess.

             I've heard so much – about you and I'm.

Shit, I'm sorry – it's just the – my car – tyres got stuck at the bottom of your drive and I had a bit of trouble getting up here and then

Chasing Clarissa – she's told you I – and she just – you've told them already I – but. No, well – she just she Runs out of the car, she Bolts like I'm a a anyway and – well you Do – and this is about a mile back and I'm there behind the fucking wheel can't see anything just keeping my hand on the bloody horn For No Reason and the wheels are jamming and it's getting a bit bloody Biblical out there and I think I I hit something – one of your chickens or something feathery and and then banging on the door and no one's answering and just starting to panic really, starting to imagine Cliss has been strung up by a bunch of fucking murderers and.

Sorry.

ALISON	bunch of fucking murderers?
SIMON	.

Yes. Well.

ALISON	Hasn't Clarissa been sweet about us to her London friends, Teddy
TEDDY	You locked the door, Clarissa
ALISON	You locked our front door?
CLARISSA	You'd left it unlocked
ALISON	You actually Locked our front
TEDDY	We never lock it
SIMON	Habit of living in London, Ted. Still. Bit weird to go round locking other people's doors, Cliss. Or were you trying to keep me out?

CLARISSA	Something like that
SIMON	You're soaking
CLARISSA	It's raining
SIMON	Inside?
CLARISSA	I'm really fine
SIMON	I've been phoning you
CLARISSA	There's not a lot of reception up here
SIMON	I tried the landline – your landline, Ted
TEDDY	Oh
SIMON	Just rang off. Perhaps I wrote the number down wrong?
	.
	I parked right out front, that okay?
ALISON	Not really
SIMON	Oh?
	Need me to move it?
	.
	I thought you had this Whole Bit to yourselves
ALISON	We do
TEDDY	Clarissa usually gets a taxi, you see
SIMON	Right?
TEDDY	It's the. It's the Detail. We thought Clarissa had gotten a taxi from the station like always
SIMON	I drove us
TEDDY	Yes

SIMON	We didn't get the train – I drove
TEDDY	Yes. Yes – clearly and – it's fine
ALISON	Is it?
TEDDY	He can't Hide his car, Ali
ALISON	Can't he
TEDDY	Of course not
ALISON	Why's that
TEDDY	You're being ridiculous
ALISON	Am I?
TEDDY	It's torrential out there
ALISON	Is it?
SIMON	Look, I can move it if you need me to
ALISON	No! No. No no no, I'm being Ridiculous, don't do a Thing, Brian.
SIMON	Simon.
	.
ALISON	Simon? Simon.
	How long has it been Simon? I thought it was Brian at the moment?
SIMON	No. Nope.
	No.
	Simon.
	.
	I suppose Simon sounds a bit like Brian perhaps
ALISON	No. No, it doesn't.

SIMON	Right.
	Okay. Well. Never mind.
	.
	Great. Well. It's great to be here.
TEDDY	We didn't realise that you were coming, Simon.
	.
SIMON	Right?
TEDDY	Clarissa didn't mention it.
	I think. I think we feel a little surprised. A little underprepared. A bit in shock.
SIMON	Clarissa
ALISON	She's a tiny bit mute right now.
SIMON	Okay.
	In shock?
	Well.
ALISON	Here you are
SIMON	Look, I'm. I'm sorry, I didn't
TEDDY	No. No, please don't. Let me just.
	TEDDY exits into the kitchen.
SIMON	Cliss mentioned it last month – a bit last minute maybe but
ALISON	Last month
SIMON	Yeah
ALISON	Have you been together for over a month?
SIMON	Ha.

ALISON	It's not your baby, surely
SIMON	Uh. Yep. Yeah. 'Fraid so.
	Yes.
	.
	TEDDY enters with another set of cutlery and glasses for SIMON and lays a fourth place at the table.
	Well.
	This is.
	Your place is.
	I've heard all about it, course, but really. Fantastic. Never seen a house more perfectly situated
TEDDY	It's – yeah it's. On a beach
SIMON	And you're renovating
ALISON	As you see. Teddy bought me a ladder. It's just what I've always wanted
TEDDY	You found us okay though, Simon
SIMON	Ah. Yes. Yeah. Fine. I thought the weather might set us back but we made good time – in fact, we're early
ALISON	Since you weren't invited Simon, you are especially early
	.
TEDDY	Let me get you a towel, Simon.
	TEDDY exits into the kitchen.
	.
SIMON	I've been looking forward to this lamb all week, Alison. Clarissa tells me there's nothing like it

ALISON	Does she?
SIMON	Bangs on about it every time I try to do lamb
ALISON	Oh
CLARISSA	Which is never
SIMON	I do lamb
CLARISSA	You don't
SIMON	We eat lamb
CLARISSA	That's a different thing
ALISON	Right
SIMON	Look, I feel awful
ALISON	Do you?
SIMON	I feel shit – I do – I feel like an idiot. I do understand how important today is to you all.
	.
ALISON	You do?
SIMON	Yeah
ALISON	Because Clarissa's told you all about it
SIMON	She has
ALISON	All the details and all the facts
CLARISSA	You look well, Alison. You look
	You look really well.
ALISON	And you look really fat.
CLARISSA	.
	I'm pregnant
ALISON	I know. It was a Joke.

My skin's going

CLARISSA   Going

ALISON   Feels like it's shedding. All this sea air.

SIMON   Sea air's a good thing

ALISON   That is what they say, isn't it.

Teddy's all rosy cheeks and soft stomach.

It doesn't like me.

Knows I'm a sham. Clean wellies

CLARISSA   You used to drag me out at every possible opportunity when we were small

ALISON   We're not small anymore.

It's pulling everything out of me.

TEDDY re-enters with towels. Passes some to SIMON who tries to dry CLARISSA. She moves away. He dries his hair.

SIMON   .

Proper British summertime.

ALISON   It's not normally like this

SIMON   You don't get rain down here

ALISON   When we meet – it's not / normally

TEDDY   / It's usually very bright

SIMON   Right

.

Barely know it in here though. That light – the light in here is something else

ALISON   Isn't it just

CLARISSA   It's done something to the room

45

ALISON	The removal of the staircase has done something to the room
CLARISSA	It looks right. Walls and light. It looks like it should always have looked
TEDDY	It was clear this morning. It was like stepping outside
ALISON	If I wanted to step outside, why wouldn't I step outside
TEDDY	Because. Inside is warm.

.

ALISON	Simon's really looking forward to the lamb, Teddy
SIMON	Been thinking about it all week – is that sad
ALISON	I do hope you like it pink, Simon
SIMON	Absolutely
CLARISSA	He likes it bleeding, it's disgusting
ALISON	Bleeding?
SIMON	Bleating if possible
ALISON	That's really handy
TEDDY	Slight mix up, with the dinner. I've made fish pie.

.

CLARISSA	Fish pie?
ALISON	Don't make a fuss, Clarissa
CLARISSA	But it's always lamb
ALISON	And Simon's never here and you're not normally the size of a house

CLARISSA	But it's always lamb
ALISON	And this year it's not
CLARISSA	What's the point if it's not lamb
ALISON	What's the point if it's not lamb, Teddy
SIMON	Fish is great – fish is. Fish is fantastic. Fish pie. Great.
TEDDY	Great
SIMON	Great
TEDDY	Great.
	.
SIMON	Cliss doesn't eat fish, you know?
ALISON	Cliss used to scratch her knees eating mussels barely off the rocks
SIMON	The baby doesn't like fish

.

You have to be careful about what kinds of fish anyway and what you Can eat makes her sick so.

No fish.

.

Baby Rose.

How about Rose?

We've had this top four going for ages now – what about Rose, Cliss?

CLARISSA	.

Fine. Yes. Fine

TEDDY	Can I get anyone a drink?

ALISON	We should make a start
CLARISSA	But there's not really any
TEDDY	Lunch isn't far off
SIMON	Cup of tea would be great
ALISON	We've had tea and we should move onto the wine now
SIMON	Uh. It's a bit early – I'll be out if I
ALISON	Well, yes, everything's a little early today. A glass of wine, Simon?
SIMON	Uh. Right. Okay. Okay, yes, sure. Yep. Weekend after all
TEDDY	There was a mix up with the lamb
SIMON	Okay sure, why not
ALISON	Good
SIMON	A glass of red would be
ALISON	White. We always start with white.
SIMON	.
	Okay. White it is then. Course – with fish.
	I bought a very nice Chablis, open that
ALISON	We have wine already.
SIMON	Okay. Okay.
	Cliss said not to bring a bottle – said that there was A System but. Well. You can keep that for another time – my Dad'd do some real grave turns if I showed up without wine, was the sort of thing he'd, you know, learnt that's what you Do and
TEDDY	We always have this wine, I hope it's alright

SIMON	Course. Sure it's great, it's all just great.
	.
	Lovely.
	.
TEDDY	Your father's dead then Simon
SIMON	Yes, he
ALISON	Teddy, you forgot about Clarissa
TEDDY	What
ALISON	Clarissa needs something to drink.
TEDDY	Oh. Course. Sorry – my head is
CLARISSA	It's fine
TEDDY	Lemonade or um juice or something? Or there's tonic or
ALISON	She can have a glass of wine, Teddy. Clarissa Always has a glass of wine.
	.
SIMON	Well. Best not to. With the baby
	.
TEDDY	Ribena? I think we've got some Ribena
ALISON	Since she Always has a glass of wine, Teddy, perhaps you should pour her a glass of wine
SIMON	Clarissa doesn't really drink anyway
	ALISON laughs.
	And I'd really rather you didn't.
ALISON	Teddy.
	We're being rude.

Clarissa will feel left out.

Teddy.

TEDDY pours a glass of wine.

They say it's not a problem. Later on in pregnancy

SIMON   Well. No, that's not technically – we don't actually fully understand the risks at the

ALISON   Because there aren't any

SIMON   No – again, that's not technically – and. I think it's best. It's best if we just avoid it. Altogether.

ALISON   She.

           .

SIMON   Sorry

ALISON   You said it's best if We avoid it. You appear to be drinking. You mean She.

           .

SIMON   I'm not really sure that's the point

ALISON   When did you become a We Clarissa? You've always been such an I.

           Here.

           .

SIMON   Cliss –

           .

CLARISSA   It's fine.

           It's not a big deal.

           It's just a glass.

           .

She sips it.

TEDDY I ought to check on the pie. Really isn't far off.

     Doesn't take very long.

     So. Shouldn't be much longer.

     Might even be ready.

     .

     Al. Can you give me a hand?

     TEDDY exits.

     ALISON picks up the shelled peas and follows.

SIMON Right.

     .

     Well.

     How am I doing?

CLARISSA Fine. Just fine – you're doing fine

SIMON Clarissa, are you fucking kidding

CLARISSA Don't

SIMON You didn't tell them I was coming

CLARISSA I did

SIMON How could you not tell these people that I was coming

CLARISSA I did! – I just told you I did – these people

SIMON They didn't seem to be expecting me, Cliss

CLARISSA So I'm lying?

SIMON I didn't say that

CLARISSA You pretty much did

SIMON   Alright then, you told them and they're nuts

CLARISSA   Don't call her that – she's just. She's a little on
            edge.

            .

SIMON   And you?

CLARISSA   .

SIMON   You ran out of the fucking car

CLARISSA   I panicked

SIMON   Ignoring my calls, sitting there soaking wet –
            drinking?

            That's my baby – that's our baby. Rose.

CLARISSA   Don't.

            I'm not going to drink it

            I'm Obviously not going to drink it – it's

SIMON   You're soaking

CLARISSA   I'm fine

            Just.

            My head's a. You have to humour her – you
            promised – we have to humour her

SIMON   No – we're here to Fix this

CLARISSA   But she

SIMON   She might not like that, but we're here to

CLARISSA   no no no – you said. It's just a game, Simon. We
            can humour her. It's just a game and then we
            can go home.

            You promised.

            .

SIMON	Did you tell them I was coming?
	ALISON enters.
CLARISSA	I tried. I left messages.
ALISON	We didn't get a single one.
SIMON	I'm sorry
CLARISSA	I did leave messages
SIMON	I assumed you knew I was coming.
	.
ALISON	You'll catch a cold
SIMON	She's right.
	See. Listen to your, to your big sister.
	Think of Rose.
ALISON	Rose.
	Rose! Of course. Rose. Rose? Rose. Really?
	You always said you were going to name your baby Esmerelda.
SIMON	Esmerelda?
ALISON	Teddy?
SIMON	Not even a real name, surely
	TEDDY enters, holding the fish pie.
ALISON	People name their children all sorts of things. In fact. Stupid people are incredibly imaginative when it comes to naming their children
SIMON	Stupid people
TEDDY	is a bit much Ali
ALISON	What's your daughter called again, Simon

CLARISSA	It's Lyla. You know it's Lyla
SIMON	This smells fantastic
TEDDY	It's not a complicated recipe
SIMON	Who needs lamb

TEDDY is giving everyone huge portions of fish pie, forgetting that CLARISSA doesn't eat fish. When he passes plates he does so a little too noisily, a little too vigorously.

TEDDY	There was a mix up with the lamb
SIMON	So, Simon, Clarissa and baby Esmerelda?
	Not sure about that one
ALISON	Oh but you have to! Otherwise Clarissa will have a massive tantrum and never speak to you again
CLARISSA	I had a doll. And I called her Esmerelda. It was hundreds of years ago
ALISON	It was twenty-two years ago
SIMON	I just want to say. I just want to
	Reiterate how sorry I am that you didn't know that I'd be joining you.
	.
TEDDY	We. I. Appreciate that. Thank you.
	We should eat.

ALISON very suddenly raises her glass.

ALISON	Cheers!
SIMON	Course – Cheers
TEDDY	Cheers
CLARISSA	Cheers

TEDDY   We always do a cheers then

SIMON   Okay, great. Sure

ALISON   It's hardest for the first, I think – it's hardest on
             them, isn't it?

             I got my Mother's guilt – the first one gets
             this toxic combination of years of stored up
             daydreams about parenting and then this Panic
             that you're about to drop this Enormous Carbon
             Footprint onto the world and what if you fuck it
             up and everyone's got a Horror story to throw
             at you so all of this confusion, all of this Stress
             can result in some really awful parenting and
             of course the first born always gets the opposite
             of what their own Mother had done and our
             Grandmother was a bit of a / drinker, a Bit
             Fucking Nervous

TEDDY   / drinker, a Bit Fucking Nervous

SIMON   I

CLARISSA   No she wasn't

TEDDY   Yes she was   ALISON   Yes she was

SIMON   Is there a

CLARISSA   No she wasn't

TEDDY   Yes she was   ALISON   Yes she was

ALISON   But at least Prone to Handing out a cuddle
             once in a while – handing out a bit of affection
             whereas I was outside, outside on my knees in
             mud and climbing trees and told to bury ants
             and make dens and do my own tea and Make
             polite conversation with guests and Fend for
             Myself which is all fine, isn't it, it's fine – it's

SIMON   I think

55

ALISON	I think that's fine
SIMON	I hope ours will be as as uh Confident outside
ALISON	Yes! You see and then – and Then it dawned on my Mother – our Mother was not a woman who Stuck at anything you see / Remind you of anyone
TEDDY	/ Remind you of anyone
CLARISSA	Ta da
ALISON	and it it Dawned on her that she actually really craved that that
SIMON	is that, like a a
ALISON	little Doll – that sweet, terribly pretty, no fear of is this one a lesbian – which is ironic really because Clarissa is the one who has actually fucked some girls
SIMON	I
ALISON	And then along she came, along came baby Clarissa and she

Just

Caved. |
SIMON	I. Well. I'm not surprised. About that – about the girl fucking I'm a bit
CLARISSA	There was no girl fucking
ALISON	And Esmerelda had buttercup curls and a blue pinafore dress to match Clarissa's and these big big blue eyes. She looked exactly like Clarissa and Clarissa looked exactly like Esmerelda and they went everywhere together. And when Mum found wooden spoons in the golden syrup or muddy footprints in the bath or Money missing

	from her purse and Clarissa explained that Esmerelda was to blame

Everyone just laughed.

SIMON	Sounds sweet.
	Little tearaway.
TEDDY	I hope you all like it.
SIMON	Looks great, Teddy.
ALISON	What happened to Esmerelda?
	Clarissa?
CLARISSA	Could I have the peas please?

ALISON tips all of the peas onto her own plate. She takes two or three off her plate and puts them back in the bowl, passing them to CLARISSA.

TEDDY	Shall I do more peas?
ALISON	I really hate peas
TEDDY	It's not a problem. We've got a garden full of them
SIMON	Course you do
TEDDY	What's that now
ALISON	What happened to Esmerelda, Clarissa?
SIMON	Just. You're people who grow things.
TEDDY	Oh
SIMON	Wish I could do it. Very impressive
TEDDY	Aren't you a surgeon?
SIMON	No. Well. Sort of. A bit
TEDDY	But

ALISON	What happened to Esmerelda, Clarissa?
CLARISSA	We don't do that bit
SIMON	Bit?
CLARISSA	We never do that bit – we didn't – that's never what we talk about
ALISON	Today is different.
	You wanted it to be different. Didn't you? Isn't that why you ran out of Simon's car and left him at the bottom of the drive?
	Remind us. What happened to Esmerelda.
CLARISSA	I cut off her knees. I cut off her knees and I cut up her face and I drew blood in red felt tips all over her and I threw her out of the window and buried her next to the cats.
SIMON	What a terror
CLARISSA	I was about six
	I don't really remember.
TEDDY	How is everything?
SIMON	It's great. It's really great Ted
CLARISSA	What's in it?
ALISON	Fish.
CLARISSA	Specifically.
TEDDY	All sorts. Scallops, pollock, prawns
SIMON	Lovely
TEDDY	Smoked mackerel
CLARISSA	Smoked?
	Is that in the recipe?

TEDDY	Capers and some of those little um gherkin things
ALISON	Clarissa had this thing about trying to Fix things – is this fun for you, Simon?
SIMON	Sorry?
ALISON	Learning all about my baby sister – all the little bits you didn't know about
SIMON	Sure. Why not
ALISON	I came back from university once and she tried to teach me how to use a lip liner – I was studying literature, I was incredibly clever okay, Simon, I mean, vying for your Mother's affection like that can make a person tenacious and I was Bright
TEDDY	She was really very bright
CLARISSA	She wasn't That bright

ALISON	I was bright	TEDDY	She was bright

CLARISSA	And and – you come back
ALISON	and I come back, and I'm nineteen and I'm beginning to navigate the whole world really and my thirteen-year-old sister teaches me how to draw around the outside of my lips.

Do you remember?

Mum used to say she was going to Put another face on and you couldn't stop squawking it. Put another face on / fix things with another face. |
| CLARISSA | / fix things with another face.

They drink. SIMON watches. |

.

CLARISSA	Maybe we should call it Esmerelda.
SIMON	I don't know. I'm not sure about Esmerelda.
CLARISSA	I'm not sure about Charlotte
SIMON	But Charlotte was your suggestion – you love Charlotte
CLARISSA	I actually quite hate Charlotte. And Victoria. And Elizabeth.
	And Rose?
ALISON	Mmmm.
	This happens.
	A Lot.
CLARISSA	Rose is too flowery.
	Roses belong outside.
SIMON	Esmerelda?
	She'll be bullied
CLARISSA	She'll be strong.
TEDDY	How is everything?
	Is everyone enjoying the food?
SIMON	Yep, yes, it's great
CLARISSA	Dad used to make incredible fish pie
ALISON	Dad made incredible everything
SIMON	Who needs lamb
	SIMON starts to find hairs in his food.
CLARISSA	You've said that already
ALISON	Except cakes.

	He didn't think baking was real cooking
CLARISSA	He never said that
ALISON	He said it all the time
SIMON	Perhaps he just found it difficult
TEDDY	Neither of us can bake
SIMON	Clarissa made some cakes
ALISON	Congratulations
TEDDY	Neither of us are any good at baking
SIMON	She's doing really well – it's going really well

SIMON pulls a hair from his mouth.

CLARISSA	This fish is really strong – you can really. I mean, even the smell is
ALISON	Hang on everybody, Clarissa doesn't like the smell of the fish – we must all stop eating immediately and
CLARISSA	Didn't say that – I
SIMON	She's got orders for months
ALISON	Thought you weren't working
CLARISSA	I'm not – a bit but not as much
SIMON	She's employing someone
CLARISSA	I'm not
SIMON	You are
CLARISSA	Lyla doesn't count
SIMON	You pay her – it counts
CLARISSA	She doesn't want to do it
SIMON	Her rosemary loaf

CLARISSA	Focaccia
SIMON	is amazing
CLARISSA	It's – we don't normally talk about it, I'm
SIMON	I made her bake something
ALISON	How progressive of you

SIMON opens the cake box.

SIMON	Isn't it amazing
CLARISSA	I don't normally – I'm sorry – I know it's not. I wasn't thinking – I'm – don't Simon

TEDDY lifts a cake from the box. It's bright pink and blue and covered in glitter and butterflies.

TEDDY	That's incredible
ALISON	Neon
SIMON	Cliss didn't want me to bring it – didn't want to Break Tradition and – look – I appreciate I've had a big hand in that, but I thought that you should see what your sister is doing with her life
ALISON	Did you
TEDDY	I can't believe you Made that it's
ALISON	Does anyone else feel a bit Sick
TEDDY	It's Beautiful
ALISON	Bit nauseous?
TEDDY	Really impressive
ALISON	You always made little buns and fairycakes
CLARISSA	This isn't a fairycake
ALISON	My mistake. Is there a more technical term
CLARISSA	It's a. It's just a cake, Alison, it's not a

	It was silly
	You don't have to eat it
ALISON	It's very Bright
CLARISSA	It's just
	It's just food colouring
ALISON	And is it organic?
CLARISSA	No
ALISON	I thought you only ate organic?
	I thought that was your Thing these days
SIMON	It's bollocks, isn't it
ALISON	Was it when you were with a different boyfriend that everything was organic? Was that it
CLARISSA	It wasn't because of.
	It's just not something I really think about – people Change, Ali
ALISON	You always were particularly adaptable
TEDDY	You really made this Clarissa
ALISON	Teddy has never seen a cake before
SIMON	She did
TEDDY	From nothing
ALISON	From ingredients, Teddy.
	Or did you spin it from the tips of your fingers?
TEDDY	It's really brilliant
ALISON	Fairgrounds and discos
SIMON	She's being shy – she's shy

ALISON	Never used to be.
	How funny.
	I've never heard Anyone describe my sister as shy, Simon.
	And she's not normally shy when we do this.
	Though she's normally fucked so. That helps.
TEDDY	I'd be the size of a house if I could cook like that
SIMON	I'm always trying to force cakes down her
ALISON	Down her
SIMON	She's not very good at eating for two
CLARISSA	She does eat for two – I do eat for two
ALISON	She's always eaten for two. Never knew how you kept that little waist.
	You'll not get that back after Esmerelda arrives
SIMON	Well
ALISON	She won't
SIMON	Sore point, I think, so
CLARISSA	Simon
ALISON	I wonder what the sugar content is of just one slice of that
TEDDY	It's a cake, Alison. It's a cake – it's got sugar in it because it is a cake.
	.
SIMON	We were saying, weren't we, we were saying that you should do a piece. On Clarissa, on the baking
ALISON	A piece?

SIMON	Isn't that what you call it – like an article or
CLARISSA	No
SIMON	We were talking about it the other day
CLARISSA	We weren't
SIMON	We were! Something fun. I don't know, something about you sisters
CLARISSA	Simon
ALISON	Not really the sort of thing I do
CLARISSA	She doesn't do things like that – that's not the sort of thing she
SIMON	I am trying to tell them about your – about Our life
ALISON	I don't really do short pieces for anyone anymore, that's not my. And I'm not sure how Clarissa baking a cake could sustain an entire article but.
	Thanks anyway.
SIMON	Maybe you could make an exception
CLARISSA	Simon
SIMON	You ought to come and see her in action. Maybe you'd feel differently – maybe you'd see something in it and
ALISON	We don't come to London very often
TEDDY	I can't deal with it. The crowds and the. I can't get on with it, I don't
SIMON	We're not central, it's not crowded in our flat
ALISON	There hasn't been the opportunity
SIMON	There's opportunity now

CLARISSA	Simon
SIMON	There's an invitation
	SIMON has another mouthful. He coughs. He pulls a large clump of hair from his mouth. The others watch.
TEDDY	Are you okay?
SIMON	Fine. Fine. Just. Quite a bit of. Of hair.
ALISON	Hair?
CLARISSA	Or hare?
ALISON	Whose hair?
SIMON	I'm not. Look, it's fine. Really – it's not a big deal.
ALISON	Perhaps it's your own hair
TEDDY	I don't. Hair?
SIMON	Really – it's fine Ted. These things happen – it's delicious. Really
ALISON	The hair is delicious?
SIMON	It's not a big deal – I don't want to make a big thing
ALISON	Is that why you had a coughing fit
SIMON	It's really just been lovely. And. To sit down with you all and to not be elbow deep in some kid's blood for a Saturday night is a really, truly, lovely thing
TEDDY	Jesus, I'm really sorry
SIMON	Honestly, it's not a problem
ALISON	Doctor Simon Harper and the lady who bakes cakes. And Esmerelda.
SIMON	Mmmm

ALISON	How lovely
SIMON	We think so
ALISON	And the other one
SIMON	The other one?
ALISON	You already have a child
SIMON	Lyla
ALISON	Because you were married before
SIMON	I was.
TEDDY	Is she excited?
SIMON	She's thirteen. I don't think she's allowed to be excited about anything.
CLARISSA	It's not her Blood
ALISON	What a wonderful expression
CLARISSA	It's from my body. It will breathe because I breathe and take Simon further away from her
ALISON	She sounds scared
	Can't you cut her out of your life? Isn't that what wicked stepmothers do?
	You could chop her knees off.
	Throw her out of your window and bury her next to some cats.
SIMON	She's thirteen
ALISON	I don't know anything about thirteen year olds
SIMON	It's difficult
CLARISSA	The. It's the. The circumstances that surround it all. Make it difficult.

ALISON	What? That you fucked her Dad whilst Mum was at home?
SIMON	I'm sorry?
CLARISSA	Alison
ALISON	What?
	That is, factually what happened, isn't it?
	I mean. You said Circumstances, but That is what happened, isn't it
SIMON	We fell in love
ALISON	That doesn't help her, I imagine.
	Love isn't an excuse when you're thirteen.
	Or fifteen.
	Or twenty-one
CLARISSA	What're you
ALISON	She won't be comforting herself with the fact that you fell in love
CLARISSA	You can't Say things like
SIMON	It's fine. Of course she won't be. I. I'm not.
	SIMON stands.
	Your bathroom.
TEDDY	Down the hall. On your left.
	.
	SIMON exits.
	The bird.
	TEDDY stands.
	I think we might have to stop it now.

ALISON	We haven't started.
TEDDY	It isn't right
ALISON	It isn't
TEDDY	Or fair
ALISON	I agree
TEDDY	Or working
ALISON	I know
TEDDY	I love you. And I think. That we should ask them to go. And stop it
CLARISSA	He's right – Alison, there isn't any point
ALISON	Are you playing now
CLARISSA	There isn't Any Point
ALISON	I think there's every point
TEDDY	Alison
	You and me. We don't need to do this
ALISON	Don't Need to do it?
	Fuck You.
	Don't Need to do it?
	I need. I have need to do it
TEDDY	I think my head might start to fall to pieces
ALISON	I Need
TEDDY	I'm not exaggerating, I think my head might be coming to pieces
ALISON	I Need
TEDDY	Honestly, Ali, is this what you want? Because if it's what you want then we keep going, you

	know we keep going, but try to look at this with some perspective and tell me this is what you want
ALISON	What I want?
TEDDY	Is this how you imagined this afternoon
ALISON	No. No it's not actually. In my mind the backdrop to today included stairs
TEDDY	Jesus Christ. I was trying to Do Something Nice. For You.
ALISON	It's worked out beautifully – thank you, thank you So Much
TEDDY	What is Wrong with – I wanted to give you Light! Space and and light for you to move in – I wanted to find a way to lift you – I wanted your Heart to be able to Move again I wanted to take this little furious Need from its box and open it up and to give you some light I didn't mean to do anything wrong I wasn't trying to break it for you I wanted to I

I.

The bird.

·

ALISON	Had you forgotten?

·

Teddy, when you woke up this morning had you forgotten what today was?

| TEDDY | What? |

·

What?

ALISON   Had you?

TEDDY   .

           There is something here beneath my ribs which
           shouldn't be. A slide of glass in the belly of a
           fish. I can't swallow – I am finding it physically
           hard to swallow, I think there is a bullet lodged
           somewhere in my throat and that if I swallow
           that will be it I am beginning to have the very
           great feeling that the edges of my body, my sides
           and my bones have the exact same properties
           as a grenade I am constantly on the verge of
           imploding, Alison, and not only imploding but
           taking a whole fucking city down with me I love
           you.

           I really love you.

           I think about this day every day.

           There's no point to it anymore.

           Please.

           .

           .

           ALISON stands, unsteady.

ALISON   On we go.

           More wine, Teddy.

           More wine.

           ALISON exits into the kitchen.

           .

CLARISSA   Can we

TEDDY   No.

           TEDDY exits into the kitchen.

CLARISSA pours a glass of wine. She hasn't eaten any food.

SIMON enters.

SIMON   Okay. So I feel

Very much like there's something you're just not telling me and

I don't really know what to Do about that.

CLARISSA   I don't know what you're talking about

SIMON   I want. My instinct is to pick you up and take you very far away

CLARISSA   I liked that about you. That was top of the list

SIMON   Liked?

CLARISSA   When we met. I liked that.

SIMON   .

You feel far away.

Why aren't you eating anything

CLARISSA   I can't eat fish

SIMON   Anything, I said – bread, potato, salad – do you want to leave?

CLARISSA   We can't leave

SIMON   It's a little rude, but if you want to leave then we can leave

CLARISSA   You've drank about a bottle of wine

SIMON   You could drive

CLARISSA   I can't drive

SIMON   Shit, no, you can't drive, I forgot.

A taxi. We could get a taxi

CLARISSA	Back to London?
SIMON	If you wanted to do that then we could do that
CLARISSA	I can't leave
SIMON	I could have seen Lyla this weekend
CLARISSA	You leave then. If you want to. You hail a cab all the way home.
	You finish off that wine and drive into a fucking tree.
	.
SIMON	That's not what I.
	I didn't.
	I. Sorry – I.
	I can't believe you just said that
CLARISSA	I can't leave. I can't leave unless she
SIMON	She what? Gives you permission? She's not going to do that and you're a fucking adult
CLARISSA	It's her. It's just her – this is
SIMON	You know what, Her I can understand – Her, I get.
	You. You – I
	I don't know what to Do with
CLARISSA	Do with? You don't have to Do anything with me thanks
SIMON	What is Wrong with you
	ALISON enters with more wine.
	She opens them.
	TEDDY enters.

73

TEDDY	Pudding won't be long
ALISON	Cheers!
CLARISSA	Cheers
TEDDY	Cheers

They crash glasses.

TEDDY	Not long til pudding.

.

SIMON	The famous apple crumble.
	Or is it. Is it something else – have I just put my foot in it again
TEDDY	No, no. It's always apple crumble. Always.
SIMON	My favourite.
ALISON	And it's always this wine
SIMON	Great
ALISON	Which is Shit for you because it is really Shit wine that I have to keep importing from Sardinia, because that is where we got it from, even though it was really Shit, but we drank it after we'd drank all the nice stuff because we didn't care that it tasted like tin cans because we were all so very happy, I think.
SIMON	Well it's
ALISON	Here
CLARISSA	Was it hot
TEDDY	Too hot
ALISON	It was perfect
TEDDY	I got burnt ALISON Teddy burnt

CLARISSA	Where
TEDDY	On my stomach, it's scarring
CLARISSA	Did you swim
ALISON	Every day
CLARISSA	Did you eat fish
ALISON	Off the rocks
CLARISSA	Did you sleep
TEDDY	Like babies
SIMON	I don't
CLARISSA	Did you miss me
ALISON	.
	Of course
CLARISSA	Did you all miss me
TEDDY	We always do.
	.
ALISON	Have you had this wine before, Simon?
SIMON	.
	No. No, can't say that I have.
ALISON	It's a pity really. We've got a good collection.
	Well. I do. Teddy doesn't give a shit. Teddy quite likes this stuff
TEDDY	I hate this stuff
ALISON	It's from Dad. Our father was a Connoisseur, Simon. Knew his shit.

	Spent weeks building his perfect wine cellar – insulating, waterproofing, wrapping walls and cooling everything – do you remember Clarissa?
CLARISSA	Of course.
ALISON	Good places to hide, cellars.
	We used to steal bottles and blame each other.
	(Laughing.) Do you remember, Clarissa, me sneaking down there to pinch a few bottles to take back to uni – and I'd learnt a bit you know, so that I didn't steal the really good stuff – and and you were there ahead of me, taking the really, really pricey stuff?
CLARISSA	a bit.
ALISON	Sorry?
CLARISSA	Yes. Yes, I remember.
ALISON	And that time – that time, do you remember, when I came home after Dad died – I came home and you were lying in your own vomit with an empty bottle of tequila and your two front teeth missing from where you'd smashed your face – from where you'd just Thrown your face at the bottles?
	.
SIMON	Okay, look, I don't think this is fair
ALISON	None of you are being fair
CLARISSA	No. No, I don't really remember that one
ALISON	Well, no, you wouldn't. You had your own shit all up your back. No one wants to remember that
TEDDY	Ali

ALISON	Two little scars.
	Like sparrow feet. Just above your lip.
	Reminiscing.
	Once a year to tell stories.
	To share little bits of our little little lives.
	It's all fucked anyway.
TEDDY	It's not
ALISON	You want it not to be, I can see how much you want it not to be, but you can't manage it.
	All fucked.
	All fucked all fucked all fucked.
	Cheers.
	She raises her glass. TEDDY and CLARISSA do the same.
	To us all.
CLARISSA	To every last one of us.
SIMON	Can I. Can I Do something?
ALISON	I wouldn't have thought so.
SIMON	I didn't mean to make this
	I didn't mean for this to be. Any more difficult than. I'm sure it.
	I very much wanted to be here. For Clarissa, and to meet you both and to find a way to. See if we could all move forward. Together.
ALISON	Good bedside manner.
	.
	Really good bedside manner, hasn't he Teddy – you can just tell.

	Kind.
	Nice to have you on the same doorstep as death.
SIMON	I
TEDDY	I don't know how you do it
SIMON	What?
ALISON	Teddy got obsessed with this policeman whose wife had just had twin boys. He couldn't get his head around it
SIMON	Around what
TEDDY	The separation the – how you do what you do – what you said, elbow deep in blood and
SIMON	I was being stupid – I was being careless
TEDDY	But that happens – there's / blood
SIMON	/ Course it happens, course there's blood
TEDDY	And then you go home to your daughter and Clarissa and. There must have been a change when those things arrived in your life as to how you can possibly do your job – it
SIMON	No
TEDDY	No?
	But.
	No, I mean. You must think.
	Don't you.
	When a body shuts down, when all of it starts to double in on itself and it's right there in front of you and you know, you get the closest possible sense of what that

	Feels like and you must stop and think about what you might do if that were were Lyla or
SIMON	No. It's about making conscious decisions. Being practical.
	Methodical.
	Logical.
	Detachment.
TEDDY	I'm sorry. Detachment?
SIMON	It's not about me or my family or my experiences or how I'm feeling – it can't be
TEDDY	But. But. Afterwards, okay. The aftermath. That moment after somebody lives or somebody dies and you you meet their family. And they are There. These humans, these people, there
	Solid. Real. Connected to you.
	And despite all of it – all of your logic – you are now confronted with these these bodies. These living bodies and the the wreck of what has happened what they now know, the experience each of you has shared is written all over their hands and and elbows and skin – whatever you could Methodically achieve or not achieve, you must have a reaction with every bone in your body that Stays with you, that Changes you
SIMON	I go to work. I come home
TEDDY	But I. You're dealing with Everything – you've got All of it in your
SIMON	I appreciate it sounds a little
TEDDY	All of life's tragedies folded up into those briefest of moments where your face will be an abiding memory

SIMON	I don't know about
TEDDY	It will be. How do you stop yourself from becoming involved – Why would you stop
SIMON	To function. Can you imagine if I took home that grief every day, Teddy
TEDDY	There are people getting by on the hope that you remember them and feel what they felt.
SIMON	.

When I first started A&E Rotations – and I was young, okay, I was really fucking new at life – it hadn't been hard yet – there was this ninety-year-old man. Something like my third day there and no one came to visit him. No one. And I couldn't believe it, I couldn't get my – I was cursing his relatives every time I passed his bed, which happened more and more because I couldn't stand how alone he was and my own Granddad had died a few weeks before this and we'd all just fucking Crammed in to get a second with him.

He died, this man – he died and still nobody came. His face was very very grey. Covered in lines, he looked like a child had sort of. Scribbled across his face. But. I remembered his hands – one was underneath his body and the other sort of reached out a little. I remember – or, no, okay, I remember Thinking that his his fingers were shaped into the form of some other hand that wasn't there.

There were bits of of dried blood around his eyes. I don't know why it hadn't come off but it looked like someone had drawn a pair of glasses in black marker pen. Sort of made you want to laugh. Think I did.

His back was broken. His spine snapped. His bones stuck out at funny angles.

And. I couldn't fit him together. He was in pieces. I remember putting my hand into his. I remember trying to make him a whole, vivid being.

He had been pushed in his wheelchair from a balcony on the tenth storey of a high-rise flat.

.

I was Obsessed. With the details.

I Howled.

He had been alone and it was That Hand.

.

His grandson had pushed him. He had abused his twenty-five-year-old grandson for the first fourteen years of that boy's life and he'd just

Snapped.

Lost it and pushed him. Or maybe he planned it and just pushed him, I don't know.

And. I felt this enormous betrayal.

Because.

I'd sat with him as he died, this old old man and made him into something and had had Felt for him, I'd truly felt for him and Grieved for him

But also for that empty room. And grieved for some fear in me – a fear that my room would be as still.

I was Livid.

And and distraught and.

That was it. It's easy – it is instinct to reach out and to kill your own life for another's loss – it feels human, it feels natural, the way that it ought to be.

Of course it is difficult to detach. To go home and kiss your pregnant girlfriend and her bump and feel this this warmth of your own life's constancy and forget the people whose lives have just changed beyond all recognition in front of you. All of these lives hanging onto this thread, this this deeply Unnatural thread and all thoughts and memories and futures from that moment onwards blurred.

It took me years to forget his name.

.

TEDDY   What happened?

           To the grandson? What happened?

SIMON   I don't remember.

           TEDDY exits into the kitchen.

CLARISSA   You've never told me that.

SIMON   No.

           Well.

           Doesn't really matter.

           Long time ago – sorry I.

           Too much to.

           .

ALISON   Do you remember your swimming pool cake

CLARISSA   Yes

ALISON   With the chewing gum stick

82

CLARISSA	For the diving board, yes
ALISON	I got blue food dye all over my uniform
CLARISSA	Mum and Dad took the whole class swimming
ALISON	One girl lost her goggles
CLARISSA	And one boy pulled another boy's costume down
ALISON	And one girl pretended to drown and lay at the bottom of the pool
CLARISSA	For ten whole seconds ALISON For ten whole seconds
SIMON	Is there a
CLARISSA	Do you remember when Dad took us to the allotments after school and we had to stay sitting in his car
ALISON	Whilst he had a sort of breakdown and contemplated leaving Mum for
CLARISSA	We'd get sweets
ALISON	Apple bon bons. Sherbert lemons
CLARISSA	Or the laces
ALISON	Or the laces – the strawberry laces. I threaded them into those pink shoes you had
CLARISSA	You ate carrots straight from the ground
ALISON	You cried when your nail polish chipped
	TEDDY enters.
TEDDY	Pudding's not far off
ALISON	And do you remember our chickens, Clarissa?
CLARISSA	Yes.

ALISON	We had four chickens. We'd collect the eggs together.
	Esmerelda, Esmerelda Two, Bill and Ted, one, two, three four
CLARISSA	I remember
ALISON	Bill and Ted were my chickens and
	And, well Clarissa called everything Esmerelda, do you remember?
	.
	I said, do you remember
CLARISSA	Yes.
	Yes, I remember, yes yes, yes, I remember.
ALISON	Dad had to call her pea shoots and her spinach 'Esmerelda' just to get her to eat them. Because when I said my sister liked to Fix things I meant she liked to Fuck things, because she didn't mind – she really didn't mind – fucking everything up as long as she could do it her way
	.
	Do you remember?
CLARISSA	Yes.
ALISON	And when Esmerelda got eaten by the fox because Clarissa couldn't figure out how to shut the pen properly, or maybe she just couldn't be bothered, I had to give her Bill so she didn't cry. And so Bill was now Esmerelda.
CLARISSA	I was three.
	Maybe four.
	.

ALISON	You're right. Why dwell on something that happened so long ago?
	What about when you were fifteen? And I'm twenty-one? And I'm on the beach, vomiting. And I'm watching Clarissa, I'm watching
CLARISSA	We don't do this one
ALISON	And I'm watching my fifteen-year-old sister, my little Clarissa, fuck my boyfriend?
	Noise of the bird.
	It bothers TEDDY. No one else reacts.
	For the next part it is almost as though none of them can hear him.
TEDDY	Can anyone else – ?
	Is that just me?
	It's been like this for days.
	I'm tired – I'm quite tired.
	I think my.
	I feel like there's blood in my mouth but when I put my hand inside there's nothing there.
	But.
	Is it darker in here already? Is it already too dark?
	TEDDY exits into the kitchen.
	.
ALISON	Do you remember?
	Tim.
	He'd never felt that heavy on me, but on my little baby sister I can hardly see her

he's pressing down on her so much. His blue jumper is still on, do you remember that? No?

His jeans around his knees and his socks nearby. How about that?

CLARISSA   yes.

ALISON   I'm sorry, Simon and I didn't catch that – what?

CLARISSA   Yes

SIMON   Look – I don't think that this is

ALISON   Yes what?

SIMON   I don't Want you to use me for this whatever it is – I don't care about

ALISON   Yes what, Clarissa

CLARISSA   Yes, I remember

SIMON   Okay, she remembers. Let's leave it

ALISON   I took them.

Your knickers and your socks and I hung them out on the washing line.

They sagged.

I left them there until they went stiff. There were specks of your blood. And him.

Marks of him.

And I wore them. I wore your socks and your knickers underneath my clothes whilst we all sat at the dinner table that night.

I don't suppose you remember that?

CLARISSA   no.

.

He didn't seem very special.

ALISON   He probably wasn't very special. Certainly not
          special enough for you.

          *TEDDY enters with the crumble. It is very burnt. He puts
          it onto the table.*

          TEDDY's lip is bleeding.

TEDDY   Here we go.

SIMON   Are we really

          Are we actually doing this?

TEDDY   Everyone for pudding?

SIMON   No thank you

ALISON   Everyone always has pudding

SIMON   I'm not really in the mood for

ALISON   You can just leave then. If you like

SIMON   Clarissa would like to stay and.

          I would like to support that but

ALISON   Everyone always has pudding

TEDDY   *(Serving huge portions.)* You said it was your
          favourite, Simon?

SIMON   It's

          Okay. Okay.

          I.

          Alright.

          Is it – is it black, is that some kind of of chef
          trick?

TEDDY   Is it black?

SIMON	Yes
TEDDY	Bit overdone.
	It'll be fine. Dig in, everyone – everyone should dig in.
	.
	Eat up.
	We always have crumble and it's important that we do what we always do.
	Ali?
	Go ahead.
	.
	Eat.
	They eat in silence.
SIMON	Are there…peas in this?
TEDDY	No. It's an apple crumble.
	They continue eating, slowly, occasionally finding slightly obscure items.
SIMON	*(To CLARISSA.)* You need to eat something.
	.
	I'm being completely serious, Clarissa.
	Eat.
	CLARISSA takes a mouthful. She gags a little.
	She goes to take another mouthful, sees something and runs from the room into the hallway with her hand pressed over her mouth.
	Clarissa?
	SIMON looks over at her bowl –

Fucking hell – what the – ?

He runs after her.

(Off.) Cliss?

TEDDY continues to eat.

ALISON stands. Walks over to CLARISSA's place and looks into the bowl.

.

ALISON   Teddy.

Teddy your lip is bleeding.

TEDDY   What?

ALISON   Teddy, there is blood on your chin.

ALISON lifts a tiny dead bird from the bowl, looks at it, then places it back.

What happened?

SIMON enters.

SIMON   We need to leave

TEDDY   She can't leave

SIMON   Look, we need to go

TEDDY   You can't

SIMON   Look

I am hugely, profoundly, genuinely sorry for your loss. But, my girlfriend is pregnant and she is not to blame for that, Alison, you cannot punish her for being pregnant – or for anything else okay, any boyfriend fucking or chicken killing or whatever other Problems from a million years ago are bothering you here in your converted fucking barn with allotments and sea views and Scallops in your shitting fish pies and and whilst I appreciate that I can't Fully understand the situation you need to resolve, I. I need to consider her health and the baby and the stress of this is is.

I shouldn't have come

TEDDY   No

SIMON   I need to use your phone

TEDDY   You can't leave

SIMON   There is a dead bird in Clarissa's bowl there is a dead bird in the pudding there is a dead fucking bird in her dinner and one of you has fucking put it there and we therefore have to leave

TEDDY   She can't leave

SIMON   You have blood on your face

         I want to leave

TEDDY   You're drunk

SIMON   I need to use your phone. We'll get a taxi

TEDDY   To London?

         She can't leave

SIMON   You cannot keep me here against my will

TEDDY   So go.

         But she has to stay

SIMON   No. No.

         Okay? Listen. No. That's not a reasonable suggestion.

         I am incredibly sorry. For you.

TEDDY   Can I hold that?

Can I put that between two palms or carry that
sentiment anywhere? Use it for anything? Does
it have any weight or any properties that might
be useful to me – I am being completely serious

SIMON   I am. I'm sorry

TEDDY   That doesn't mean shit

She can't leave.

She can't leave.

SIMON   We're going.

*CLARISSA re-enters. She has marks of vomit by her
mouth.*

I'm sorry, Teddy. Alison.

I need to use your phone.

*SIMON goes to the phone, TEDDY intercepts him by the
table. Plates crash to the floor. Food is all over the ground.
The icing from the cake is smeared across the floor. The
men continue to struggle. CLARISSA's bowl falls to the
floor and with it the dead bird. TEDDY is tired and
soon SIMON manages to push TEDDY back and reach
the phone. He picks it up. The line is dead. He hangs
up a few times. Nothing.*

Line's dead.

Your phone isn't.

Fucking.

Clarissa. Cliss, your phone.

.

CLARISSA   What?

SIMON   I need you to get me your phone

CLARISSA   What?

SIMON	You're tired. You're upset. And this has been just.
	I'm sorry – this has been the most difficult – I'm. I need you to give me your phone.
	CLARISSA looks at ALISON.
CLARISSA	We can't leave.
	.
	He steps towards her.
	It hasn't finished yet.
	She takes her phone from her pocket.
SIMON	Give me your phone, Clarissa.
	She puts the phone on the floor.
	Clarissa.
	She steps on it with a heel, cracking the screen.
	Jesus Christ.
	What is WRONG with you?
	With all of you?
	I mean, I know what's, but for FUCK'S sake
	We need to go home
CLARISSA	We can't
SIMON	I need to go home
CLARISSA	So go.
	.
SIMON	I'm not leaving my baby
ALISON	Fucking hell

CLARISSA	Foetus
SIMON	What? Jesus Christ, Clarissa.
CLARISSA	Go.
SIMON	I'm not leaving you. I'm not, despite your – and besides, I can't, I fucking can't because none of you will let me out and this is NOTHING TO DO WITH ME *(SIMON exits into the hallway. We hear him trying to open the front door. He can't. He kicks at it. ALISON walks into the middle of the room and looks at CLARISSA.)* THIS IS FUCKING NOTHING TO DO WITH ME AND I WANT TO LEAVE, I WANT TO FUCKING LEAVE.

He comes back in.

Looks at them.

I should never have come

CLARISSA	You forgot that I don't drive
SIMON	What?
CLARISSA	And

you said I don't drink

SIMON	You don't drink.
CLARISSA	My friends think I have a drinking Problem
SIMON	With me. You don't drink with me – you have never drank with me if you have a secret drinking problem and have successfully hid that from me then that is not my fault and Why is the line dead. Have you cut the fucking line?

You actually locked me out earlier didn't you – have you cut the line

CLARISSA	That man

SIMON	Have you cut the line?
CLARISSA	That ninety-year-old man. I didn't know that
SIMON	It's not relevant. It never felt – .
	I never think about it. Never. I wanted to – share something of. I'm drunk and you're all being fucking needy it seemed like the Appropriate thing to
	I don't think about it
TEDDY	Is it darker in here?
CLARISSA	Does Beth know?
SIMON	What?
CLARISSA	Does Your Ex Wife know that story?
SIMON	Of course she does. She was there – what the hell does that matter? I didn't Know you then, Jesus, Clarissa, we're still getting to know each other
CLARISSA	I've got something of yours inside me and we're still getting
SIMON	You know, contrary to how this afternoon's gone, there are some things we should discuss in private
CLARISSA	I think everyone's well aware you've had your penis inside me, Simon
SIMON	It wasn't important! That story didn't mean a thing, I can't believe you're making this about you
TEDDY	It's dark again.
CLARISSA	Sometimes I think this baby will come out with plastic shoulders and plastic knees and fluffy yellow hair and I'll colour her in with felt tip

	pens. Give her big eyelashes. Chop off her knees with scissors. And throw her out of a window
SIMON	For God's sake
CLARISSA	It never really kicks.
	It doesn't move.
SIMON	She. Not it.
CLARISSA	I wondered if perhaps it isn't real.
	I wish that sometimes.
	I think about hangers.
SIMON	Fuck you.
CLARISSA	.
	Molly.
TEDDY	What time is it?
ALISON	What did you say
TEDDY	Why is it so much darker already?
CLARISSA	Molly.
	I think about Molly.
	.
ALISON	Do you?
CLARISSA	Yes.
SIMON	I feel sick.
ALISON	What do you think about?
CLARISSA	All
ALISON	Yes.
CLARISSA	Her. A new little person in the world.

You. Suddenly allowing yourself to be soft.

Her noisiness. Me. Being an Aunt.

An awful Aunt.

Not very there.

I was waiting til I could give her advice on boys.

Which is an odd way to think about a four-year-old.

ALISON   What else?

CLARISSA   I'm tired, Alison, I'm

ALISON   What else do you think about?

CLARISSA   Being

here.

Taking sanctuary in your big warm heart of a home after another breakup, another fuck-up at university.

You cuddle me.

We eat lamb. Crumble.

Drink white wine that's too posh for the occasion and far too early in the day. It's wasted on me and I say so but you want to look after me and treat me and you and me drink it til it's all gone

ALISON   All gone   CLARISSA   All gone

CLARISSA   and we have to have the shit stuff from Sardinia and you're all brown and it tastes lovely because our smiles are too big for the cheap tannin to get to.

	We joke about tequila – it is funny that I smashed my teeth in

ALISON   And look how perfect they are now – have another glass

TEDDY   Is it raining – they're very white

ALISON   It's never raining   CLARISSA   Fill her up

TEDDY   Did it cost   ALISON   Ummmm
            Tequila?
            a lot of money

CLARISSA   A Fortune – bit more   Teddy
                                       – what's Tequila?!

TEDDY   Ummmm

            Tequila

ALISON   A Bad Bad kind of

            Juice? Juice – can we

CLARISSA   That is sort of like Wizard Nectar because it makes everything awful disappear

ALISON   Don't say that!   TEDDY   Please don't say that

CLARISSA   it's funny – it's funny I smashed my teeth in because I haven't fucked-up on that level since, I am trying to be a Grown Up here and you are indulging me

            We joke about chickens.

CLARISSA   One, two, three, four   ALISON   One, two, three, four

ALISON   She left the pen open

CLARISSA   I did   TEDDY   Clarissa…

            I was Heartbroken – and and being a brat

ALISON   Your little face – you were so forlorn, how could
             I not – that lip

CLARISSA   This lip

TEDDY   Clarissa how could you

ALISON   That lip

CLARISSA   Allotments and sweets and I tell Molly all about
             Esmerelda – the nice bits not the horrid bits
             because I want her to only think of me as kind.

             She sits upon my knee.

             She joins in, it's lovely, it's annoying, Teddy's
             wrapped up in her. You roll your eyes.

             Later you lie on your kitchen floor, your legs
             stick out at odd angles, you have sick on your
             chin and you moan and you look how I must
             have all those years ago. Except your child is
             missing and I had just wanted to get Fucked.

             .

             I'm standing on a beach. On your beach.

             Barefoot.

             She takes her shoes off.

             And it's. It's five years ago.

             And it's five years ago.

CLARISSA One two three four five	ALISON One two three four five	TEDDY One two three four five

CLARISSA   My hand is holding a littler hand. Always on a
             beach, always in a hand, my hand bigger this
             time. Her little hand her little hand her little
             hand, fingers sticky from jam is in mine.

ALISON   Slower.

98

CLARISSA   She stamps out shapes in the sand in her frog
            wellies. We stamp together.

            CLARISSA stamps in the food.

            And she's chattering through her little pink
            O-shaped mouth and my drunk lipstick is on
            her cheek from big fat kisses and she's bounding
            cheeks popping and she's beaming from the
            very middle of her the very centre of her little
            self. Hallo world hallo world hallo world.

            And it is. It is five whole years ago.

            .

            She's skinny legs and pointy elbows. And we're
            running.

            *CLARISSA runs around the table, her bare feet in the food
            and on the broken plates. Her feet bleed.*

            We stop

            She stops.

            And we sit

            She sits.

            And she lies upon my tummy

            She lies down.

            And I can't feel the point at which she starts and
            I stop and I wonder if that's what it feels like. To
            have a belly full of another a whole world within
            what I had thought was only mine to keep, to
            change, to mark. And I can smell lavender and
            bonfires and.

            and

            .

            and

.

And then it's something different.

She's uncovering every rock, every shell. She's shooting for the dead boats behind the old shed and then. And then it was that something stopped. For some for some reason I can't end, everything changed.

I wasn't with her for four minutes. Maybe five. Some days I swear on my life it was only one second. Other days I remember it was weeks.

I time it in my head.

I think the same thoughts.

I go to find her.

It's a game.

But she isn't.

She isn't there where she is supposed to be.

She isn't anywhere.

My ribs were bruised from where her elbows had dug into me.

I pressed upon those bruises and when they faded I cried again. A new grief. A new loss. A new guilt.

Over and over and over and over.

She limps at me in dreams.

Her legs seizing up from cold and she is bent double, her arms bright, her heart dizzy, her eyes drunk and she is always reaching for something beyond me. She beams at me from waves blue and white from water.

She's in the sand, she's in fields of heather, nests of crows, nettle ditches, abandoned skips and countless letterboxes. Everything is lost to me.

Wherever there should just be an empty space, there she is. Knotted.

.

TEDDY	Where did you go?
CLARISSA	Back to the house.
TEDDY	Where have you been?
CLARISSA	Back at the house
TEDDY	Why did you leave her?
CLARISSA	For a
TEDDY	Why did you leave her?
CLARISSA	I didn't
TEDDY	Why did you leave her?
CLARISSA	I don't
TEDDY	Why did you leave her?
CLARISSA	For a cigarette – I didn't want her to
TEDDY	Where has she gone
CLARISSA	I don't
TEDDY	Bring her back
CLARISSA	I'm not
TEDDY	Make her here again
CLARISSA	Please don't do
TEDDY	Get out
CLARISSA	Teddy

TEDDY   Get out quicker.

CLARISSA   I.

                .

               Sound of the bird again. TEDDY *is again bothered by it.*

ALISON   She couldn't sleep on her own.

               That's what won't go.

               I feel like you've left her in some room with a
               chair and no window and a sixty watt bulb and
               she's wondering why we don't come.

               Silence.

               ALISON stands, legs nearly giving way.

               She goes to the telephone.

               CLARISSA takes a step. Her feet are bleeding.

CLARISSA   Alison

               *ALISON sees the cable is not connected to the wall.
               Connects it.*

               She presses the answerphone button.

AUTOMATED
VOICE   You have thirty-eight messages.

               Beep.

                .

ALISON   What?

AUTOMATED
VOICE   First message. Received Wednesday 24th at
               6.43pm.

               Beep.

CLARISSA's
VOICE   *(Through answerphone.)* Alison. Teddy. Hi.

So. It's Wednesday.

And it's nearly Saturday.

It's Clarissa, by the way, but I guess you.

I'm bringing someone. Not someone, Simon.

Simon.

He knows. He knows the. The necessary bits.
So. I am appealing to your generous nature.
And because he won't – . And because Simon is
Normal. Normal and sweet and and Good and
Good to me and Dull and. He's coming.

I'm in a bar.

I am Very fat.

Call me back.

Please.

.

Click.

ALISON presses a button.

AUTOMATED
VOICE   Next new message.

CLARISSA's
VOICE   Me. Again. My head hurts. Call me

AUTOMATED
VOICE   Next new message.

CLARISSA's
VOICE   Call me back. Call me back call me back
             call me back

AUTOMATED
VOICE   Next new message.

CLARISSA's
VOICE   It isn't fair. It isn't fair. Call me.

AUTOMATED
VOICE   Next new message.

CLARISSA's
VOICE   I'll keep calling. I'll just keep calling

AUTOMATED
VOICE   Next new message.

CLARISSA's
VOICE   You're being FUCKING UNREASONABLE
            by the way

            ALISON unplugs the phone.

CLARISSA   Look, I

ALISON   Teddy.

            Have you left the phone the whole time?

SIMON   Your feet are bleeding.

ALISON   You should go.

TEDDY   It kept ringing.

            On and On.

            You kept ringing and ringing and ringing and
            ringing.

            I've only ever wanted to make things Right for
            you, Alison.

            Every year.

            Feels like we're just losing her again.

            Every year.

            I gear up to it.

It never feels like five years ago four years ago three years ago two. Feels like now.

ALISON   I want it to feel like now.

TEDDY   My hair is literally falling out and into food.

And my hands won't Do for the thing that is anything and

They won't stop, Simon you said you killed a chicken.

He goes to the floor by the food.

Looks like the sea doesn't it – looks like a drawing like the sky and the sea and the fish and the birds and is it very dark in here.

I haven't slept in three days and there is blood in my mouth I feel like I've been eating glass. Three nights I stared upwards.

The bird is loud again, constant.

Can anyone else hear that? Here that hear that? Which is it? Hear that?

ALISON   Teddy

TEDDY   Am I making any noise?

.

Am I making any noise?

ALISON nods.

CLARISSA   I feel a little faint.

Simon. Could you get me some water?

.

SIMON looks at her.

ALISON goes into the kitchen. SIMON goes to the phone.

TEDDY stands.

He has cut his hands very badly. There is a lot of blood.

SIMON picks up the phone.

TEDDY exits into the hallway.

SIMON dials.

SIMON   Hi. Number for a taxi near.

Near. Near – I don't. Hang on.

We hear the sound of a door being opened ever so quietly.

A postcode – let me – I don't know, just hang on a second

.

ALISON enters from the kitchen with a glass of water. She gives it to CLARISSA.

ALISON   Where's Teddy?

SIMON   *(To ALISON.)* What's your postcode?

ALISON   Where's Teddy?

CLARISSA   I don't know

ALISON   Where did he go

CLARISSA   Out the front, he went in the hall

SIMON   Postcode, what's the postcode

ALISON goes to the hall way

(Into the phone.) Yep, bear with me, I just need to double check

He looks for post on the phone table.

E…X – it's it's up a lane   ALISON *(Off.)* Teddy? Teddy?

Hang on a – 11, EX 11, 1D4

ALISON comes back in

ALISON   Front door's open.

              ALISON looks at the floor. Registers the blood.

CLARISSA   Alison.

ALISON   You can go now

CLARISSA   I don't want to leave like this

ALISON   I need to find Teddy

CLARISSA   He'll be outside

ALISON   You wouldn't leave it alone.

              You couldn't leave it alone.

CLARISSA   I wanted to help all of us move on I wanted to

ALISON   For yourself.

CLARISSA   We should talk. All of us

ALISON   I don't think I need to see you anymore

              None of this. None of it was how it was supposed
              to be – none of you could manage it. Why is it
              easier to forget it all? Why doesn't anyone want
              to still feel it? Want to push on that bruise?

              Where is he?

CLARISSA   I am sorry

ALISON   You're not. Otherwise you would have just
              borne it.

CLARISSA   I'm sorry

ALISON   You're sorry it's been difficult for you.

CLARISSA   I miss you.

ALISON   You should leave. You can leave. Free to go.
              Get out.

CLARISSA	I'm lost
ALISON	That has nothing to do with me
CLARISSA	I need you
ALISON	I don't understand what that means

A banging begins offstage, quite faint at first, but it gets increasingly loud. Nobody notices at first.

ALISON	I wonder why you came
CLARISSA	What?
ALISON	Seriously. Why? Why show up at all?
CLARISSA	Because. Because that's what we
ALISON	We we we we we what? I don't force you here. I don't hold you at gunpoint. You hassle and you wail and you whine and you're not sorry. You don't Feel sorry.
CLARISSA	This is the only time you'll see me. To remember Molly.
ALISON	Rolls off the tongue.

Don't say her name.

Don't say her name with your stomach. This giant belly. So full. Full of something you don't need or want.

You should just leave.

Off you go.

CLARISSA	Alison
ALISON	You are going to make a terrible mother, Clarissa.

Suddenly there is a big crash. Bits of the back wall begin to cave in.

They all turn to face the wall and disperse further apart. The crashing continues and a big hole in the back wall grows. An overwhelmingly bright light from outside begins to flood the stage.

The hole gets bigger.

TEDDY's silhouette can be made out. He is covered in bits of plaster, his hands are covered in blood. The noise becomes constant.

The noise stops. TEDDY stands still.

ALISON Teddy.

Oh.

What are you – ?

TEDDY It was my hands. They couldn't stop. They felt like meat.

And my heart. It was my heart – it wouldn't Wouldn't stop.

It's this light Ali!

It's the biggest, most incredible thing. And it keeps banging into things, they keep getting in the way and I keep thinking that if we just if we just if we just If we just if we just if we open it up a bit, we could let it all out. All of this light.

And it won't be…knocking into things.

ALISON Teddy.

Teddy, my love – what are you doing?

TEDDY I haven't really slept.

In three days.

Maybe four.

I've tried shutting my eyes. But it's like I can't. Physically do it.

Three days.

And I'm lying there.

And then.

And then

And then it was ten.

And then it was ten.

And then it was ten years ago.

And it is ten years ago.

It's ten years ago and it's two o'clock in the morning and I'm having a bath. I'm having a bath and I've finished all my marking and I want a bath to stop my bones from dropping out to keep my eyes open and I'm having a bath to put myself back together. And you have on this dress, this light light dress that pulls in at your waist and falls low on your back and all of your hair is up on your lovely lovely head and the whole room is steam.

I'm in the bath.

I'm in the bath.

And you're stepping out of the dress and into the bath all at once and I want to hold your hands that are on your little stomach as you tell me. Your bright bare shoulders and your beam from the very middle of you as you tell me and I hold all of you. I hold your head and your back and your stomach and your arms in one go and everything that I had hoped for is contained, locked in you and your stomach.

.

And then it was six years ago.

And it is six years ago.

Molly.

These big, proud, round letters on leather handbags and around skirting boards and staircases in purple crayon.

And she's loud. She sings. She sits on my shoulders and she's funny. She's the funniest person that I have ever met. I have a new name. A short name that smacks of something happy

Dad

And she's happy and she's big and she's filling rooms in a bigger room in a bigger room in a house and we are one two three happy.

And then.

It's five years ago and she's gone.

I find a purple crayon Molly in tiny letters behind the fridge and I can't stand up for a week.

And it's four years ago and I can't remember.

Her weight written as a number and her shoes that we keep in the cupboard in her room that wouldn't fit her anymore and her funny little smell and the knowledge that she loved Ribena and the photographs of her that we keep in drawers for your self preservation won't combine to create anything real.

She's lost. And seems to be found only in radio waves and television reports that are less frequent now, less supportive now, less there now.

And you're gone. You're gone.

And it's three years ago and you're more
vanished than she is building scaffolding on any
memory I have of you and it's two years ago and
we're here. Playing a game.

Eating lamb drinking wine talking about
chickens about fucking chickens grasping details
telling stories blaming blaming and you're so
angry. I can't find mine. You're bile and rage
and I am hopeless. Unable to hold you with
shaking hands and arms that drop every time I
try to lift something up.

.

Sometimes.

Sometimes in the small of the morning we find
each other in late dark early light.

You make yourself very little and I weep and we
tuck into each other saying her name somehow
trying and failing to make something new and
we stop lying and we grieve.

.

And.

And. This year. This year is different.

I can't sleep.

And you've left you've gone and I think you've
left notes there's so much more that

I'm supposed to Do this year. I have to make
something I have to make the lunch but it's too
dark I can't find anything. I know it's the same
– I know that everything must be as it always is
and I know that you think this is the biggest way
to say I love you now. I love you now. I love you

now. I love you now. Doesn't mean as much on
such well practised lips.

Four days ago and you've gone.

And the phone won't stop screaming.

And the birds won't stop ringing.

Three days and I'm not sleeping I'm driving.
I'm driving at three am to get the lamb to get
the fish to get the flowers to get the wine to get
the peas but the phone won't stop screaming
the birds won't stop ringing and I don't think
I worry that I can't do this that it's not right to
do this that this is the one day the one day a
year when it's your turn to fracture to break to
splinter and mine to hold you up but that I'm
not really holding you or helping you like you
are my very life source now, but that I'm letting
you drain yourself to pieces.

And it's now.

And there's a bomb in the room.

And you're further away from me than you have
ever been.

Somctimes I thlnk I might die if you never look
at me again, that way you used to and that way
she used to from the very very middle of you.

And it's one year away. And I'm not playing.
I'm not pretending. I'm not here. And you're
not here and there is a different family here, a
different set of lives here. And we're paint in the
walls. We're the floorboards and we're the stain
that you left from leaning on too many walls the
wrong side of windows just waiting. Just waiting.

But it's two years away. And it's two years away.
And I am tired. Tired because I am beginning to

feel something close to happiness again. You're wearing new blue dresses and cooking again and I am growing vegetables. Simply growing vegetables.

Away from the sea.

Away from the sea.

TEDDY is on the floor. Exhausted.

ALISON holds his head in her hands.

Black.

by the same author

Revolt. She said. Revolt again.

in *Midsummer Mischief: Four Radical New Plays*
ISBN 9781783191574

You are expected to behave...

Use the right words

Act appropriately

Don't break the rules

Just behave

This play is not well behaved

Alice Birch examines the language, behaviour and forces that
shape women in the 21st century and asks what's stopping us from
doing something truly radical to change them.

Winner of the George Devine Award for Most Promising New Playwright 2014

Many Moons

ISBN 9781849430777

'...an absolutely incredible script. It's rare to see a play and be so sure that
it will stay with you for a while but *Many Moons* is precisely that...
An incredibly tense, dense and tight play... Beautiful, and slightly terrifying.'
British Theatre Guide

'This is a meticulously written play...that slowly turns you inside out.'
The Guardian

'Birch's writing is poetic and rich with imagery...
it's a confident and exciting piece of writing...
as a marker of things to come, it's one to remember.'
Exeunt Magazine

WWW.OBERONBOOKS.COM

Follow us on www.twitter.com/@oberonbooks
& www.facebook.com/OberonBooksLondon

Milton Keynes UK
Ingram Content Group UK Ltd.
UKHW021113021124
450589UK00014B/1147